The Ultimate Essay Guide

Sam Loyd & Justin Moryto

ISBN-13: 9781983169991

CONTENTS

ACKNOWLEDGMENTS

Writing a book is not an easy task – trying to write something that has been written about countless times and in numerous ways makes it just that little bit harder. When we came up with the idea for this book, we decided we wanted to put a useful spin on the essay writing genre. Whilst the book may focus in on essay writing it also has many tips and trick, strategies and *hacks* that students can use to drastically improve their university academic life.

But of course, we wouldn't be here if it wasn't for a few select individuals that have helped us craft this unique specimen of a book...

So thank you to Scott Taylor for talking through the idea with us, and giving us invaluable insight into self-publishing.

Thank you to Lynn Hamilton for undertaking the mammoth task that was editing this book. *It is, after all, made in the edit.*

Thank you to our early readers who's feedback was invaluable in making this book what it is.

CHAPTER ONE: INTRODUCTION

Writing essays can be a daunting task, especially if it is your first proper university essay. There are significant differences between essays you write at school and those you write when in higher education. These differences stem mostly from the sophistication of argument, the level of research, the quality of referencing and the time spent sweating with nerves waiting for your results.

There are further differences, however, in terms of length and style. Essays written in North American universities tend to be shorter, require less in-depth argument but are required on a more frequent basis than in European institutions. In the latter, particularly the United Kingdom, students have fewer essays to write but they are required to dive deeper into the subject. This book is aimed more at the task presented by the European style essay. Although most of the tips, tricks and methods are universal, especially the note taking, planning and exploration of the question, the research and writing techniques may differ slightly.

So, if you are a North American student coming to the UK for a year abroad then be prepared to do more research and be more focused with your writing. If, on the other hand, you are heading out across the Atlantic, be ready for a higher frequency of assignments but a reduced workload for each individual essay. Demands vary around the world but, generally, essay writing fits within one of these two main models.

What is this book designed to do?

This book has been written as a guide for students when writing essays. The art has been broken down into the main aspects of essay writing, using actual student experience rather than one specific professor's point of view and combined into a general-purpose guide by people who have been to university in the last five years.

You can read it in one sitting, and try to absorb all the information as you go, or work with it as a companion guide and refer to it naturally at each stage. Of course, you can stick it on the virtual shelf and only pull it down when you're really stuck. We don't mind as long as it helps!

Throughout the book there are also links to useful external resources. If you are reading the e-book version, then you should be able to click on these links; with the hardback version, a quick Google search may be required. We have also created some resources, unique to this book, for our readers to use. These include:

- Planning templates
- Reference cheat sheets
- Note-taking templates
- Submission formatting templates

These resources can be found at www.currikula.com/ultimate-essay-guide-resources

Book overview

Question

The first thing to tackle with any essay is the question, whether that is dissecting the one that your professor or teacher has provided or creating your own. The latter is almost always the most challenging.

We'll take you through analysis of the question by looking at sample questions – how you can break them down and go beyond those common terms like "explain", "critically analyse", and "explore" and use them to maximum effect. We'll also look at methods for crafting your own questions and the pitfalls to avoid during the process.

Research

When it comes down to research, being able to access the most relevant and important sources quickly and efficiently is always a priority. No one ever complained about *not* having to read irrelevant articles or books. To fine tune your research capabilities, we look at practical ways to optimise your use of the library and increase your reading speed as well as systems you can use for scanning text. We'll also share some of the top online tools and an offline system that helps to prioritise your reading and source the most valuable documents to inform your essay content.

Note-taking

Being able to research and read lots of relevant sources for your essay topic is next to useless if you can't find an effective way of storing the information. If you have an eidetic memory, then congratulations, you can pretty much ignore this section. However, if you are not blessed with such gifts, then we have many tricks and tips that allow you to make effective, high value notes. It is then only a short step to the creation of an essay plan that almost writes itself or arms you with the notes that allow you to enter the exam room with great confidence, which might be a new experience for some of you. * We also list a tonne of different tools that you might want to use to further facilitate the process.

*Disclaimer: *the essay won't actually write itself and we can't guarantee confidence – sorry!*

Planning

During our university studies, we found that if students spent time constructing a decent essay plan rather trying to write 'off the cuff', it actually cut down the time taken to write the essay, improved the quality of writing and led to an overall increase in grade. If you know the direction you want to go and how you'll get there before you set off, then there is little chance of getting lost, having to pull a 180 and go back on yourself or simply end up at a dead end with no finish in site. That being said, there are people that love to freestyle, get excellent marks, and write remarkable essays without ever putting pen to paper or finger to keyboard, to make a plan. The words slide across the page as smoothly as a figure skater cruising across the ice rink. There are some people who can write a first-rate essay in 24 hours without batting an eyelid. If, however, you are not one of these aliens masquerading as a human, then planning meticulously is probably the path for you.

We'll also touch on the structure and the building blocks of an essay, how to break these blocks down and arrange them to write almost any style of essay quickly and effectively.

Writing

Writing is structured. Writing is best when there is variation in sentence length and complexity. Writing is helped by formats and standard practices that improve the readability and quality of your work. Here, we'll look at the classic - "point, quote, explain" – a simple approach that is absent in many students' work. We'll delve into how to formulate an argument effectively and how to maintain a logical, consistent and valid argument throughout your essay. And, finally, we'll look at some of the dos and don'ts of essay writing.

Editing

Once you've written your essay, the last thing you want to do is read it again and again. Depending on your deadline, you may be lucky and be able to take a few hours away from staring at your words and come back to it with a fresh eye. Whatever your time frame, many authors admit that their books are made in the edit, forged in the fires of cuts, rewrites and restructuring. Whilst you may not be writing a book, even though a dissertation may feel like one, the same metaphor applies. If you've closely followed a well-structured plan, these edits will be minimal. If not, then there's every possibility a surgeon's steady hand will be needed to cut away the superfluous words and distracting ideas. We highlight some of the tools available to help you edit and improve your essay.

Referencing

Perhaps every student's least favourite aspect of essay writing is the referencing section. We tackle this behemoth by dissecting the main types of referencing you will encounter: Harvard, APA, MLA and Chicago. Whilst we cover the majority of elements you may want to reference, very niche things - such as a particular podcast or earnings call – have been left out as they would take up far too much space and, quite frankly, we wouldn't recommend doing it by hand anyway. We'll give you a link to download cheat sheets for these giving you a quick way to implement the most common forms and point you towards tools that remove some of the effort and make referencing a significantly faster experience.

Presenting

Finally, when your essay is complete, there is just one final task – preparing it for submission. A well-crafted essay needs to be presented properly and most universities have set standards or styles that you need to follow. Although they are all generally the same, it is worthwhile checking with your professors or having a quick look at your course guide to see if they highlight the specifics for your course or department. There are rumours of one or two people trying to hand in an essay written in the comic sans font... they were never heard from again.

Anyway, enough with the overview. But, before we dig into the middle of this essay writing sandwich, we have a few more general tips and tricks that you might find useful during your time at university.

General Tips and Tricks

Browser Recommendation

Everyone knows there are many different types of web browser out there. However, one of the best, if not the best, is Google's Chrome. This is mainly down to it being the most widely used browser in the world which has the effect of it being fully supported by almost every site. This means that websites will look like they are meant to, features will function correctly, and services will run (competently) 99% of the time.

But, more importantly, Chrome lets you add browser extensions. Other browsers have similar functionality, we are not denying that, it's just that the Chrome eco system for browser extension is more diverse and has many more options, allowing you to augment your browsing experience.

Procrastination

We all procrastinate. This section is devoted to the time spent procrastinating instead of editing this book! But there are tools and strategies that you can use to reduce the amount of time you spend being distracted, looking at social media or simply not focusing on the task in hand. We've outlined a few of them below for you to check out... and procrastinate from reading the rest of this book.

Pomodoro Technique

This technique breaks up your work into smaller, more manageable, chunks. Traditionally, an egg timer is used but there are apps now available that allow you to set an alert for say, 25 minutes in the future, and then you work until that time is up. When the buzzer goes, you take a quick 3-5-minute break before embarking on another 25-minute segment. Ideally, this is repeated four times in total before giving yourself a longer break of around 30 minutes.

Focuswriter

This program removes the distractions from your screen when you are working. It's a word processor (like word) that simply blocks out the back ground so you cannot be distracted by other windows. You can also set alarms and timers to make sure you stay focused for the required time.

URL

https://gottcode.org/focuswriter/

Freedom App

This is one of the best distraction-blocking apps out there. It works with Mac, Windows, iPad and iPhone so there is little excuse not to use it. The app blocks your selected sites for set time limits leaving you to work undistracted. Users say they gain an extra 2.5 hours of productivity each day whilst using the app. Think how much more you could accomplish in a day!

URL

https://freedom.to/

And of course, feel free to check out www.currikula.com/ultimate-essay-guide-resources for other tools aimed at helping you achieve better grades.

CHAPTER TWO:
THE QUESTION

Introduction

Nine times out of ten, when your professor sets you an essay, it comes in the form of two things: a word count, just how much do you need to write and, secondly, a question - the cause of weeks of anxious debate about when to start working, what to write about, and whether or not you can have another drink at the bar and then start it tomorrow.

There is, of course, the possibility that the professor doesn't give you a question, just a topic. Normally, the topic will relate to aspects of the course you're studying and he asks you, the student, to come up with the question. These are fairly uncommon in your first year of university but they will probably increase in frequency as time goes on.

- **As an aside, once you get the hang of coming up with your own question they are the best option - you can write the essay in almost any way and with the most freedom.**

In this chapter, we examine the different types of question you might receive, the common words that give you a clue as to what type of question it is, and finally some tips on formulating your own question - how to frame it to fit what you want to write about.

But first...

How long is your essay?

This is important. It indicates just how deep you need to go into the question. It guides you on how many people you need to include in a discussion on a topic and how many points of view are required for a counter critical analysis. We will delve into this far more in the structuring section, however, a cursory look now never hurt anyone.

Generally, essay length falls into three brackets:

< 2000 Words

If your essay requirement is sub 2000 words generally you're in a good place, as there isn't too much space to bring in a lot of in depth opinions. This reduces the workload and makes it easier to focus on the main sections, bringing in auxiliary authors, critiques, perspectives or explanations as needed rather than setting them up as full blown counter-arguments or alternative positions.

2000 - 5000 Words

This bracket is rather large. Essays nearer the 2000-word mark may resemble their lower word count brethren in approach, however, as a rule of thumb, they will most likely need a minimum of two opposing or critical views developed in length. Deep analysis of quotes, arguments and how they fit together with other external critical analysis will be required in many cases.

5000 > Words

Essays of this length are approaching dissertation or thesis level and will require significantly more research and a generally broader, but still as deep, discussion of the topics raised by the question. It can take significant time to delve into the question if one has been set or, more than likely with essays this length, the question will be up to you. If that is the case, then, as we outline later, the question isn't as important as correctly planning and researching your essay.

Types of Questions

There are many different types of questions and they all have their own little caveats and nuances that are not always strictly adhered to but they do provide guidance on what you should be writing about. Every subject will also treat these questions slightly differently. Sadly, this is also true for professors. So, we would advise checking with your professor once you have chosen the question you want to answer. You could even take it a step further and share your plan with your professor to guarantee that what you write will be what they are expecting to read.

Overall, there are considered to be two types of question - critical and descriptive. Critical essays are those that analyse and critique the topic in question, whilst descriptive essays are those that simply explain the topic. Naturally, it is rare that questions are purely one or the other. We have identified five question categories that cover these two types (see next page):

Analysis (Independent)	Analysis (Personal links)	Comparative	Critical Explanation	Explanatory
Analyse	Assess	Compare	Clarify	Define
Critically evaluate	Comment upon	Contrast	Demonstrate	Describe
Evaluate	Consider	Examine	Elaborate	Explain
	Discuss	Review	Explore	Give an account of
	Identify		Show how	Illustrate
	Interpret		To what extent	Outline
				State
				Summarise

However, this table doesn't accurately show the overlap between the subjects and types, often they are much closer than this table suggests.

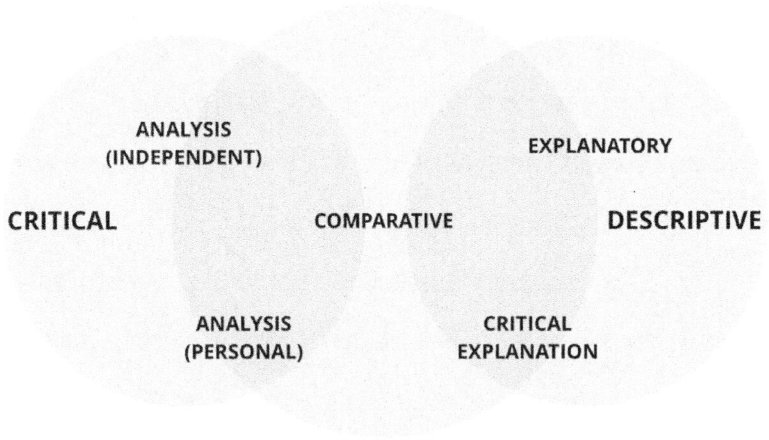

ANALYSIS (INDEPENDENT)

EXPLANATORY

CRITICAL

COMPARATIVE

DESCRIPTIVE

ANALYSIS (PERSONAL)

CRITICAL EXPLANATION

All question categories contain some degree of critical analysis and description and the longer the essay the far more likely it is to involve both.

Analysis (Independent)

These questions can be defined not only by their need for detailed analysis of the given topic but also the requirement that all conclusions reflect others' critiques or supporting arguments. This means, importantly, that whilst it requires your input, the arguments and analysis are drawn from other critics, and you simply provide the glue that holds them together. You are wielding the critic's sword rather than doing the critical cuts yourself. It doesn't mean that some level of analysis isn't done by you, it is normally confined to the conclusion and leans heavily on the correctly cited work of others.

- **Important:** These essays are rarer than those that require your personal input and development of more opinionated conclusions.

Example Questions

- Does evil raise an insurmountable problem for the theistic conception of God?
- Critique Freud's concept of the ego using Carl Jung's works.
- Analyse the role of Joseph Goebbels in the Third Reich.

Keywords

Analyse

When you analyse something, you break it down into its core parts, examine their relationship to each other, and delve into how they build up and form the whole. If an essay question asks to you 'analyse' a particular topic, argument or position your professor will be expecting a level of deconstruction within the essay.

Once you have achieved this deconstruction of the essay, you should look at debates both for and against the core parts you have identified during your systematic break down. The shorter the essay, the deeper you should look at singular core issues and their respective arguments. The more words you have to play with, the more likely you are to be able tackle the topic as a whole.

Critique

When critiquing, it is often assumed that some level of understanding about the topic has already been established. Therefore, the only explanation you need to offer is that related to the deeper criticism and insight you are making about individual points.

If you are asked to critique a well-known argument as part of your topic or question, then it will be easy to find counterpoints, create discussion and delve deep into both the logic and structure of the argument. These can be used to show views that are both for and against as presentation of a well-balanced essay is important. However, making sure the side you agree with and believe in survives the counter arguments is also key.

Justify

Justification falls into both types of analysis. In this, the independent version, you may be asked to justify an opinion or argument using other people's work on or around the subject. Building a solid argument that is based on this supporting evidence is more important than presenting your own evidence or supporting arguments. As always, it is important to work with arguments that are contrary to the main thesis of your paper and examine them in a balanced way.

Analysis (Personal critique)

These essay questions require a similar approach to those described above, but do require a greater level of personal input. They want you to be part of the critical analysis, using others' arguments to support your overall thinking on the subject. They expect you to formulate an argument that is supported by the evidence and research of others.

- Discuss the relation between narrative style and moral judgement in Joseph Conrad's Heart of Darkness.
- Discuss with examples how and why major international actors have been perceived as failing the victims of genocide.
- Assess the new insights in the understanding of Haemolytic Uraemic Syndrome and its worldwide implications following the large scale outbreak of E.coli O104:H4 diarrhoea in Germany 2011.
- Evaluate the effect of World War Two on the economies of France and Great Britain during the 1950s.
- Critically evaluate the role of Henry VIII's annulment to Catherine of Aragon in the formation of the Church of England.

Keywords

Analyse

Analysis of these questions is very similar to the description above; they just require more of your own input and personal direction over where the essay's overall argument will lead.

Critically Evaluate

A critical evaluation of a subject warrants an assertive essay describing, in detail, the extent to which you agree with a set of findings, a theory, or an argument. It is important to note that you will need to provide ample evidence to support your claims. Furthermore, you will need to make sure your analysis is balanced by presenting a critique of alternative perspectives. With this essay style, you are trying to convince the reader to take your side of the argument, to sway them to your perception of the topic. Come to a final conclusion, basing your decision on what you judge to be the most important factors and justifying how you have made your choice.

Assess

'Assess' questions are all about weighing up the extent of truth about a particular statement or position. You are expected to consider or make an informed judgement about the value, strengths or weakness of an argument, topic or claim. It will involve taking multiple, different viewpoints into account in order to provide breadth of discussion. When reaching the conclusion, it is best to clearly state how far you agree with the original position, taking into account all the alternatives you have considered.

Consider

Say what you think and have observed. Back up your comments using appropriate evidence from external sources or your own experience. Include any views that are contrary to your own and how they relate to what you originally thought.

Discuss

This type of question distils down to a debate on paper; it requires you to use reason and logic to go back and forth between arguments. You must bring in arguments, counter arguments and counter-counter arguments as you discuss the topic. All your points must, of course, be carefully backed by evidence and supporting views where applicable. It is important to have your conclusion in mind when writing this essay as it will help to keep you on track.

Examine

A question that uses the key word 'examine' is less exploratory than some of the other types of question we've discussed so far. Here, you are expected to focus on a particular piece of evidence and analysis to inform your critique. There is less of a debate/discursive theme to this style of essay as you are required to focus intently on analysing the source content provided.

As this is a critical evaluation, it is important to look closely at this source material and establish key facts and important issues surrounding the topic to ensure you have a good understanding of the role and effect it has in its environment. This is key to writing an effective and quality analysis of the subject. Providing context for your analysis is encouraged and naturally comparing your findings to other scholars will go a long way to elevating the level of your work.

To what extent

This question is asking you for your analysis of the topic in question. It wants you to delve deep into the subject matter and evaluate how far you agree with the proposition. As with all critical essays, evidence is required to support your views and it is paramount that you display the extent of your knowledge (the more research the better). Remember to consider both sides of the argument before presenting a conclusion that is logical i.e. it follows on from the arguments and counter arguments. Ultimately, you must show why a particular set of evidence, or piece of information, has greater validity in supporting your answer.

Justify

As with the previous scenario, you are making a case to support an idea or point of view. However, in this version, it is more likely to be your own idea or your own argument that supports that view. This should obviously be backed by supporting evidence, but the focus is less on the extent to which other arguments support your view and more about how you use that evidence to argue your point. Remember to critically analyse your approach and your arguments in order to provide valid and fairly presented criticisms that, through good analysis and counter argument, you can overcome.

Critical Explanation

Probably the most common form of essay, requiring you to not only demonstrate your knowledge of a topic but also provide a critical analysis of it. They are very common in History, Politics, Psychology, subjects where you are required to explain a theory, event, or a decision and then subsequently analyse it, critique its effects, debate the causes or something similar. Be wary of falling into the common trap of spending too much time on explanation and not enough time on critical evaluation as this could severely limit the marks your essay can achieve.

Example Questions

- Explore the meaning of 'radical evil' and the 'banality of evil' and how they might relate to understandings of evil using the cases of Idi Amin and Adolf Eichmann.
- Conjectures and refutations by Karl Popper (review essay).
- To what extent do Hobbes and Locke differ on the distinction between the state of nature and the state of war?

Keywords

Demonstrate & Show how

Both 'show how' and 'demonstrate' require you to present, in logical order and with relevant evidence, the stages and combination of factors that give rise to the subject of your essay. They require examples that illustrate your points and accurately 'show how' something has arisen from the different factors. Remember to follow the principles of cause and effect and don't miss out the middle step when showing how 'a' becomes 'c' ('b' in this case).

Elaborate

Elaboration can be used in both a critical and a descriptive way. You may be asked to expand on a topic by simply giving more in depth information or you may be asked to expand on a criticism of a topic and delve into counter arguments.

In both cases, it is important to remember that, when providing more detailed information about the subject in question, you need to be adding value to the discussion with information that has not already been stated. This is a double-edged sword, as you must also make sure you stay within the boundaries of the original discussion. In other words, keep the topics you expand relevant to the original source material.

Explore

Exploration in an essay can, at first, appear slightly confusing - how does one explore within text? However, the confusion quickly clears if you understand that what they are really asking is for you to look into a variety of different viewpoints and, where possible, reconcile opposing views by presenting a final line of argument at the end.

Your argument shouldn't interfere with the series of consistent and unbiased alternative views you present around the subject but remain objective during the tour of topics as much as possible. As you near the end, you can start to focus the exploration towards the conclusion that you believe to be best.

- **Pro Tip:** A detached tone can be helpful as it will keep you from including your own arguments until the end and reduce the chance of being seen to favour one argument over another too early in the essay.

Identify

These questions are normally looking for you to describe the 'key points' that lead to 'x'. Whilst they stem from descriptive questions, a level of analysis is required to ascertain which of the points/factors/premises/etc you need to identify.

Occasionally, there is a direct stipulation to analyse this afterwards. It goes without saying that it should be supported with evidence and valid argument-based discussion. Make sure you maintain high levels of coherency in order to avoid confusion about which 'key points' you are identifying. These are meant to be specific and shouldn't be generalised. i.e. don't take one half of an argument as a point or be selective about the premises you choose.

Interpret

Interpretation is asking for a direct critical opinion on a subject. You can be asked to demonstrate your understanding of an author's particular terminology or what the findings from a piece of research suggest to you. In the latter, comment on any significant patterns and causal relationships between subjects. You are being asked to come up with a 'reading', a 'view' on a matter. It is normally important to find supporting views, or contrasting ones to compare and analyse the interpretation you are presenting.

Comparative

Comparative essays are pretty much as the title suggests. You are being asked to take two or more ideas, arguments, topics, subjects or theories and compare them to each other. There are varying levels of self-analysis required for these kind of essays, generally governed by your professor or setting. For example, in an exam setting, more self-analysis with brief supporting quotes or evidence from other scholars will be enough. However, if it's a term-time paper, then greater weight should be put on backing up your analysis with more in-depth use of other scholars' published work.

Example Questions

- Compare the developing situation with North Korea and the United States of America and the early days of the Iran Nuclear deal.
- Compare and contrast the viability of nuclear powered rockets to their more traditional chemical counterparts.
- Review the effects of Russian influence on Eastern Germany in the 1960s, 70s, 80s and how it has impacted commercial development in the area.

Compare

Traditionally, 'compare' is nearly always accompanied by 'contrast', however, if it is not then you need to look at the basic facts relating to two topics and try to find similarities between them. Then, you need to understand the roots of these similarities and to what extent they contribute to making the topics resemble one another.

If 'contrast' is included in the question, then you are also expected to include elements of that key word.

Contrast

In direct contrast to compare, 'contrast' is looking for the differences between subjects. What are the main dissimilarities? What sets them apart? Try and break these down, as before, into the core components and compare them. Comparing both subjects at a higher level is a good starting point as you can dig deeper into the subjects as you delve deeper into your own essay.

Review

Review is included here because a reasonable element of comparative analysis is undertaken when reviewing. To write a good review, you need to convey the main points, placing emphasis on global structures and interrelationships rather than going into minute detail. In effect, summarise the material you are reviewing and highlight the main points you plan to comment on later.

Then, you will need to comment logically and analytically on this material. Pose yourself some of these questions: what have other researchers said about the subject? Are there any views that contrast with yours? What do you agree or disagree with? What evidence are you using to support your assessment? Make sure your line of argument is running through the essay, clearly showing which side you support.

Explanatory

Explanatory essays are perhaps the most simple in concept, but also quite difficult to perform well in. If it is your first series of essays, it can be difficult to explain content succinctly and with clarity. Below are some of the words that normally indicate the need to be more explanatory than analytical.

Example Questions

- Clarify the processes required to enrich uranium.
- Define the relationship between Prince Charles and his mother, with relation to the effects on the British Monarchy.
- Describe the 'Special Relationship' that the UK and the US has with one another.
- Explain the effects of the Chinese economic policy in the 1990s and how it has led to their global position today.
- Give an account of the ways David Cameron failed to plan for the EU referendum in 2015.
- Illustrate the role of phosphorus in plasticisers, flame retardants, and pesticides.
- Outline three of the main causes of the Palestine conflict.

- State the main benefits of having a subsidised and free health care system.
- Summarise the difficulties of staging a traditional war with North Korea, from a US perspective.

Keywords

Clarify

This means to provide insight into a subject and, quite literally, provide clarification. For example, this could be done by explaining an argument or topic in simpler terms. Coherence is an important contributing factor to getting those higher grades. Remember to present your answer in a systematic manner.

These questions require you to shed light on a topic or, in some instances, break down a complex subject into simple parts and demonstrate how they all fit together. The clearer you can be, the better the result.

- **Pro Tip:** Once you think you have grasped the tricky concept try and explain it to a friend. Getting someone else to understand can help you to see where the difficulties may lie.

Define

Here, you must outline the precise meaning or understanding of the subject. Most of the time you will be asked to 'define' one element in relation to another. This narrows down the question and hopefully allows you to be more specific. Check with your professor if the question seems too general.

Further, if the definition you provide is contested, i.e. there are opposing views, then make sure you raise them. Some questions to ask yourself include: How have others defined the subject? Why is it contested and why have you chosen to use one meaning instead of the other if this is the case? Providing more than one view on the subject will show that you have a greater grasp of the literature and go a long way to improving the quality of your work.

Describe

A 'describe' question focuses less on the basic understanding of something like an event or a situation and more on its particular characteristics. These should form the building blocks of your answer to the question. Provide a detailed explanation as to how and why it occurs and recount this in your essay.

Explain

Similar to 'clarify' and 'describe', you are aiming to give a detailed account as to how and why whatever you are writing about occurs or what is meant by the use of this term in a particular context. Your writing should ensure that complex procedures or sequences of events can be understood. Define key terms where appropriate and substantiate with relevant research.

Give an account of

Similar to 'explain' or 'describe', meaning to give a detailed description of something.

Illustrate

These questions tend to require graphs, figures, tables, statistics or other concrete research to support them. Check with your professor if you are unsure about what is suitable to include. The aim is to use these tools to demonstrate your knowledge of the subject and intertwine with data to support your points relating the question. The data should be used to help clarify your point rather than confuse.

Summarise, Outline & State

All of these follow a relatively similar set of requirements - condensing the information into its core parts. Trimming the fat of the topic so to speak. There is no need to be overly descriptive and it is best to avoid waffling on about non-essential points.

There needs to be a condensed, but organised description of your topic. Important supplementary information that improves the reader's ability to understand the subject is important but minor details are not. Brief and general examples are helpful to illustrate these points. The key is to communicate all the main facts to the reader in as punchy and succinct a manner as possible.

Two-Part Questions

The two-part question is a particular favourite of professors, always hoping to get the most from their intrepid students. They may present as two connecting questions or as a paragraph of text followed by two posed questions.

The first step is to check for multiple key question words. If there is more than one, then the questions may be asking for different things in each part and it is likely that you will be required to combine them in some way.

What do we mean by this? You may have to explain the causes of topic A in relation to analysing the effect they have had on topic B for example. Or you may be required to review the work of scholar A in contrast to the work of scholar B.

- **Note:** Multiple key question words can be easier as they will allow you better demonstrate your knowledge and writing ability.

It is important to try and determine if there are any unstated parts to the question. For example, if there are two questions on a subject, it is highly likely your professor is guiding you towards a specific answer. Several authors may have commented on these exact questions or they may be an extension of a lecture you had earlier in the term. It is always worth taking your time to try and figure out exactly what the question giver is asking and how you think they would want you to respond.

Next, you need to determine how much of the word count or exam time you are going to devote to each part of the question. If there is a descriptive or explanatory part and a critical analysis section, how much are you going to write about each?

Our suggestion would always be to do about one third on the descriptive side, and then two thirds on the actual analysis. Professors nearly always want a quick demonstration of your basic grasp of the concept before you share your analytical reasoning and your reading around the main subject. This second, analytical part, is where you can really show how much work and effort you have put in by bringing in arguments and analysis of other authors and using them to support or criticise your line of argument.

If the two parts of the question appear too different and don't seem to connect properly then we advise you asking your professor for clarification, choosing a different question or reading further around the subject to see if you are missing the link. It is very unlikely that **part b** of a question will not have a reasonable relationship to **part a** and, therefore, could be a sign that you have misinterpreted the question.

Creating Your Own Question

The trials and tribulations of coming up with your own essay question at the outset seem rather daunting. Where do you even begin? What do you think you want to write about? Can you change once you've started? How long should the question be? How specific do you need to be?

Well, luckily for you, we have a relatively simple strategy to solve all these problems. First up, you need to realise the question doesn't need to come before the answer; the answer can quite neatly define the question.

What does this mean?

It simply means that you can write your essay before you write your question i.e. define your question through what you have written. Before you get in a muddle trying to wrap your head around this concept, here is a little comparison.

When something really amazing happens in your life, one of those life-altering stories where maybe you brushed so close to death that, had you been wearing any baggier clothing, the reaper himself would have managed to drag you into his domain. Or, perhaps where success came at the last possible moment, snatched from the jaws of defeat, in a way almost no one would believe.

These kind of stories deserve titles, they are not your run of the mill night out, growing up story, they are more special than that, and thus they are named. But they are never named before the event takes place. It is the event that creates the name. Where would you begin to try and name something that hadn't happened yet?

Obviously, there are quite a few flaws with this analogy. But the basic lesson is valid. Sometimes the only way to name something is to experience it. Expecting parents spend months debating the name of the child, to only pick one and, on the day, when they hold their newborn baby in their arms, they throw the name out the window because it no longer feels right.

How should you go about this?

The first step is figuring out what you want to write about. This can be quite difficult if you have a completely free reign but generally you have some limitations presented by the subject you are studying. That being said, if you have an issue or favourite topic you want to write about, nine times out of ten you could probably twist an aspect of your course in such a way to enable you to do it.

Once you've tied down your topic, you then go through the research, planning and writing stage. However, before you get to the editing stage, you need to pause with that first draft is sitting nicely in front of you, waiting to be polished to perfection. And it is here that you come up with the question or title of the essay.

Of course, it doesn't have to be a question in the traditional sense, you could come up with a title and a subtitle. This is more typical of longer essays as they cover more depth; a simple question could be harder to relate back the content or the relevance may not be so clear.

Remember your question or title should accurately reflect what you have written. If it is a question, it should be related to the root cause of your chosen line of argument. If it is a title, it could be the name of the debate you participate in or perhaps it is presents your primary argument with a new twist. Naming can be hard but, like many things, once you get the hang of it, it becomes easy.

- **Note:** It is rather rare to write your own question and just write an explanatory essay. If you are not sure this is what you are supposed to do, then check with your professor. The longer the word count required the far more likely a decent, if not greater, level of critical analysis will be required.

CHAPTER THREE: RESEARCH

Introduction

Now you can better understand the essay question you've been set it's time to start looking for the information you need for the answer. This process can be tedious. It is often made worse by procrastination as who wants to comb through hundreds of pages of dense academic text... well some people do and that's fine. In fact, lucky you, your life is significantly easier than those that find it hard to concentrate and keep track.

One thing to bear in mind is that your approach to the research will differ according to your familiarity with the topic. If you are not particularly familiar, the process is more likely to be one of discovery and involve broader research than if you already have a decent understanding. A greater understanding of the topic will allow you to be far more specific with your research. The benefits are multiplied several times over if you know enough to sketch the barest of plans.

- **Pro Tip:** Pick a topic or a question where you have a reasonable general knowledge so that you can minimise the 'discovery phase' of the research.

This chapter starts by outlining a couple of "pre-researching skills" - things we've found that may improve the speed and quality of your research and allow you to not only blaze through documents faster and with better accuracy, but also allow you to passively research whilst you engage in something else.

Following that, we share some of the best methods to comb through texts looking for relevant and important information. And, lastly, we have the "recommended" section, where we share all the best sites we've used to find articles, books, and information as well as other general places that are a good starting point for research.

Pre-Researching Skills

Speed Reading

What is Speed Reading?

Speed reading is the simple process of improving your ability to read by as much as five-fold! Seriously, most people read at an average of 200 words per minute. But, with practise, you could find yourself easily doubling if not tripling your reading speed in a short amount of time.

Speed reading is probably one of the most overlooked tools in anyone's arsenal, just cutting the time it takes to read books or articles in half saves hours and hours over the course of a week and days over the course of a year.

We'll be honest though, it's hard, hard work to practise and maintain. You may see a doubling in your reading speed in the first couple of hours but, if you don't continue practising, then you'll lose the skill and any chance of further improvement will be lost.

- **Note:** This works for people with dyslexia as well.

How does it work?

There are three primary things that drastically increase your reading speed.

1) Decrease fixations
2) Eliminate regression
3) Increase horizontal peripheral vision

Decrease Fixations

Perhaps, surprisingly, you do not read in a straight line, but rather in a sequence of jumping movements. Each of these jumps ends in a 'fixation' or a snapshot of the text on which you have focused. This snapshot is around the size of a 20 pence piece from eight inches away (average reading distance). These fixations all last from around a ¼ to a ½ of a second in an untrained eye. Thus, reducing the number of fixations per line decreases the amount of time your eyes spend on each line and therefore decreases reading time.

You can feel these jumps for yourself by closing one eye, putting your fingertip on top the eyelid and, with the other eye, scanning a horizontal line (as if you were reading). You should feel that that movement isn't smooth, but jumpy. This doesn't work if you make a massive jump, i.e. shift your eye from one end of the line to the other without scanning the middle.

Eliminate Regression

Regression is also known as backtracking, relooking at what you have already read. This can be conscious (low comprehension of the text's intended meaning) or subconscious (misplaced fixations [snapshots] of the text with your eyes). Tackling conscious comprehension is hard and doesn't offer the largest gains in reading time. However, missed fixations cause you to read 25% slower.

Increase Horizontal Peripheral Vision

When you look at the words on a page, you normally focus on one word plus the next in the sentence and that is all you process before moving on. However, if you can harness your peripheral vision, that is the objects at the edge of your vision, then you can take in larger parts of a line of text at once, reducing the fixations (snapshots) and upping the number of words you process per minute.

Techniques to Learn

General

It is suggested that you should practise at between two to

three times the reading speed you wish to accomplish. So, if you're looking to achieve 400 words per minute then somewhere between 800 and 1200 words per minute should be your target practise reading speed. Practising above and beyond what you want to achieve will help you adjust to the new speed of reading faster.

You will also need to establish a baseline to check your progress. To do this, choose a book that you haven't read before to use as your practise book.

Calculating a baseline

Open to a standard page (not an introduction, or a page half filled with a picture/diagram) and **count the number of words in 5 lines**.

Take that number and **divide it by 5** to get an average per line.

68 words / (divide) 5 lines = 13.6 (rounded to 14) words per line

Then count the **number of lines on 5 pages** before **dividing by 5** again to get the **average number of lines per page**.

143 lines / (divide) 5 pages = 28.6 (rounded to 29)

Then multiply your **average words** by your **average lines** to get the **average words per page**.

14 X 29 = 406 words (average per page)

Now mark your first line. It doesn't have to be with a pen, just do it mentally, and find a device on which to time yourself (your phone, or Google "timer") and set it to **60 secs**.

Then, **reading normally (avoiding the temptation to read super-fast**) and with the intention to **comprehend as much as possible** from the text, start the timer and begin.

When the timer is up, stop and then count back from the line you were on to your starting point. Take this number (total lines read) and multiply it by the average words per line you calculated earlier. This should give you a baseline value for your normal reading speed.

How to Decrease Fixations and Eliminate Regressions

Trackers and Pacers

Trackers and pacers are great tools for forcing you to read faster. Don't worry, you don't need to buy these, a pen or pencil works well. Start by taking the end of the writing implement of your choice and placing it under the first word on a line. Slowly run it along the page with your eyes focused on the tip (cap on, no need to ruin a good book) and the words right above it.

As you progress down the page, start moving the pen faster and faster. This is effectively the core part of the exercise you're going to practise repetitively to improve your speed.

Technique

Firstly, it is important to get the technique right. The first mini exercise showed you the simple principles, now it is time to nail down the specifics. You're going to want to spend a **maximum of 1 second** on each line with the pen.

- **Pro Tip:** Do not concern yourself with comprehension. We repeat. **DO NOT** CONCERN YOURSELF WITH COMPREHENSION.

The focus of this exercise is to train your eyes to move faster, to decrease the fixation time and reduce regression. If you can, increase the speed as you move from page to page. Do this for **2-5 minutes,** until you feel you are comfortable holding the book and moving the pen.

Once you have mastered this, it is time to move on to the speed improvement part of the exercise. This should last for **3 minutes**. Make sure that you practise rather than just daydream. (This is a real problem if you don't focus). During these 3 minutes, each line should be processed for a **maximum of ½ second**, that is 2 lines in the time it takes to say "one-one-thousandth".

Again, it is vitally important that you do not concern yourself with comprehension, doing so will slow you down. At these speeds, you may not feel like you're taking anything in. That is fine, it is not the goal of the exercise to comprehend the text. The goal is to become far quicker at processing the words on the page.

Perceptual Expansion

This practise approach is similar to the one used when trying to increase reading speed. You will use your tracker/pacer (pen) to run along the page, at a speed of **one line per second**

as before. However, this time you will **start from one word in** and **end one word before the end**. This is because you don't want to waste time 'comprehending' the margins as they are of little use. With practice, this technique can triple your reading speed as you cut down drastically the number of fixations you undertake per page. Take the sentence below for example:

"This | is a sentence of twelve words and stretches across the | page."

You would start from the indicated mark " | " and end at the same mark " | ".

Advancing

To increase the effectiveness of this exercise you should steadily increase the number of words in from both the start and the end of the line, i.e. going from 1 to 2 up to a maximum of 3. Again, this is not about comprehension, in fact you may not comprehend anything, it is about training your eye muscles to move faster and quicker.

The more you practise, the better you will become. When you no longer find it too much of a challenge to read through pages like this, it will be time to test your baseline again.

When you do this, you must revert to reading without the tracker/pacer but as fast as you can **whilst still comprehending the text.** This is different from what you have been practising and you shouldn't expect to read at the faster speed as that was focused on muscle improvements rather than comprehension. After repeating the baseline test, tally up the lines you've read in the same one-minute span and see how well you've done.

- **Pro Tip:** After you've successfully increased your reading speed, keep practicing to maintain the improvements and read even faster.
- **Pro Pro Tip:** Focus on your comprehension when needed, if you're speed reading texts looking for relevant information to help your argument, you can sacrifice a little comprehension to get through enough of the text. However, if you're looking to understand a valuable piece of text, then slow down a little to improve your comprehension.

*** Some of this information was sourced from Tim Ferris's article on speed reading.**

Reading Apps

We've not been paid to endorse these, they are simply the ones we have used or know are useful.

Spreeder

The Spreeder app is designed to train you in the art of speed reading. It flashes each word of a sentence on the screen in front of you. It does a good job of demonstrating just how fast you can read. They also have different training modules although some of these cost money.

URL

https://itunes.apple.com/gb/app/spreeder-speed-reading-e-reader-and-trainer/id1110276339?mt=8

ReadMe!

ReadMe is similar to Spreeder, but specialises in making your eBooks quicker to read. It has a synchronization feature that allows you to sync your content across devices if you are willing to pay the monthly fee. It works well on an iPad or similar size tablet.

URL

http://www.readmei.com/

Outread

Outread is great for news junkies just wanting to keep up with current events as it allows you to sync with other popular news reader apps data. You can also use the highlight function to focus on the word you are supposed to read as it goes along rather than the single word at a time.

URL

https://outreadapp.com/

Currikula's Speed Reader

A chrome extension that allows you to quickly read through information on the web. It has 'skim read' functionality allowing you to get the gist of the text even faster. Power through all your potential resources for your essay in half the time.

URL

https://chrome.google.com/webstore/detail/currikulas-speed-reader/llfhifhjokjallcnpkmfcjfmadmbchcl?hl=en

Websites

Free Reading Test

This is an online free reading test that not only tracks your words per minute but also tests your comprehension. It has varying levels of difficulty with regards to text content so you can practise at multiple different levels.

URL

http://www.freereadingtest.com/

Readsy

Readsy is a simple, no nonsense reader that scrapes the text from websites and allows you to read it quickly on their page. You can also upload PDFs or text documents to speed read. It uses the similar idea of displaying words quickly on the screen.

URL

http://www.readsy.co/

Auto-Narration

Ever listen to an audio book? Stephen Fry and the Harry Potter series perhaps? If you've never experienced an audio book or some form of auto-narration then we'd suggest you change that now. Never has it been easier to absorb information whilst doing other things. Load up a book that you need to read on your phone and have it read to you as you go about doing pretty much anything else.

Auto-narration is slightly different from audio books as it aims to take text and transpose it into audio. This opens more doors to what you can listen to but, whilst some apps are getting better at synthesising the human voice, there are still a few hurdles to overcome. You can be sure that within a few years these problems will be solved and any piece of text will become effectively an e-book read by a professional narrator.

Where to get audio books?

Librivox

You can get lots of free audio books from Librivox – a non-profit initiative to produce audio books from those available in the public domain.

URL

https://librivox.org/

Audible

Perhaps the best known, Audible has thousands and thousands of books on demand that are read by professionals and ready to consume on the go. Whilst there is a monthly cost, if this proves to be the best method for you to learn about your subject, it may just be worth it. There is a 30-day trial available, allowing you to test it out for free.

URL

https://www.audible.co.uk/

Apps/Websites for Auto Narration (Text to speech)

Natural Readers

Natural Readers allows you to upload documents and text and then synthesise one of 57 voices for you to listen to. It is also free to use (20 minutes' worth of content a day) and has a slick interface. (They also have an Android and an IOS app.)

URL

https://www.naturalreaders.com/online/index.html

TTS Reader

TTS Reader is similar to Natural Readers, except with a smaller range of voices. It doesn't have a 20-minute free tier limit though! So, you can listen to your heart's content.

URL

https://ttsreader.com/

ISpeech

An app for IOS that reads text back to you, supports all major languages and you only have to pay if you want different voices.

URL

https://itunes.apple.com/gb/app/ispeech-text-to-speech/id322329515

How to find the best resources

Having discussed different methods for absorbing the content of the resources that you've found, we should probably focus on the actual finding part now. We've outlined below a few different methods that can help you achieve your goal which is, of course, to find the most relevant and useful information for your assignment as quickly and efficiently as possible.

Using your professor

Your professor, the person who set you the task of writing this essay in the first place, is always a good place to start. Ask them if they have any recommended reading on the subject. Ideally, you should have some idea of how you want to tackle the question or topic before you ask. The more specific you can be with your questions about recommended reading, the more specific (and time-saving) their answers will be. Make sure to have the notes section of your phone handy, or a good old fashioned bit of pen and paper, to capture what they say.

- **Pro Tip:** Check the course materials for a reading list first. It's a good place to start and, if you are unaware of its existence, your lecturer may not be too impressed with your lack of devotion to the subject.

Using your class notes

There is a good chance you will have covered your essay topic (or at least some element of it) at some point during the term. This is especially common in the first couple of years at university. Go back to your old lecture notes, or borrow someone else's if you were "ill", and look for authors and commentators that have offered opinions. These will be a great starting point for delving further into the debates around the topic and the notes could well nail the basics of the essay.

Using your friends

Got friends on your course in the year above? They may have written on the same subject, drop them a line and see if they can't give you the 101 on what you need to know or who you should read. Friends in your year on the course may be of help, but only if you're trailing behind them in the research phase. Also, we offer no guarantee that they won't tell you to go away for being lazy and not doing your own research. You may have to try the noblest of traditions and bribe them with food.

Using online forums

Sites like Quora or Yahoo Answers offer potential sources of expert opinion. Want to know more about your subject, or find specific responses to arguments? Then post questions here. This tactic, however, does require some early planning as there is no guarantee that you will receive prompt answers.

Reddit also has an active community and your subject may have what is called a subreddit, a smaller, specified niche forum for the topic, for example, www.reddit.com/r/philosophy. However, Reddit can be a double-edged sword as you can end up spending hours browsing random content rather than finding specific resources.

The Student Room has a pretty active forum community as well and doesn't run the risk of dragging you into unrelated cat videos. Check out https://www.thestudentroom.co.uk/forum to see the whole list.

Using alternated cited works

If you already have some set texts for your project, or have used other methods to assemble an initial reading list, then you can use this technique to quickly expand that list. At the end of all proper academic texts there is a reference list/bibliography, something you will be familiar with given that you have to include one in your work as well.

This is a relative gold mine - a list of sources that someone writing on a similar topic to you has used to prepare their own academic text. Often the text will cite the source during its main body, allowing you to easily identify what is useful and what is not. For example, with Harvard referencing, following a quote you will see the reference (Howes, 2012). If that quote is useful, or you think that author of the quote may have other useful information, the bibliography/reference list at the end of the text will contain all the details on the resource allowing you to go and find it for yourself.

How to properly use a search engine (Google)

We all think we know how to use a search engine... enter the search terms, maybe even stick in the author of the article we are looking for and, *voila*, there is a direct link to the paper. And this works quite well, most of the time. But what if you're not looking for a specific article? Searching for "Alternate theories to Pierre-Simon Laplace's tidal flow" presents us with a myriad of results, including Laplace himself, but not much of a focus on the contrary commentary. So, how can we use Google to do a better job and get to the results we want faster?

How Google ranks your search

Firstly, it is important to know how Google ranks your search and, then, how you can take steps to eliminate relativistic criteria that will impede that search.

Google ranks your search with hundreds of criteria which include but are not limited to - where your search terms appear in the document and how frequently, the popularity of the page in question, or the "authority" of the page on the matter. However, you can change the results by simply changing the order of the search terms, meaning that how you phrase a query is as important as the query itself.

Further, the country that Google thinks you are in will affect the results. For example, if you have a VPN saying you are in Albania when you're actually in the UK, your results will be skewered for those queries. As long as you're not researching how to dispose of dead bodies, you should be alright turning off your VPN during the course of your research. However, if you insist on using a VPN, then you could also try navigating to the subdomain version of Google of the country that is more relevant to your query. These can be found at this URL: https://www.distilled.net/blog/uncategorized/google-cctlds-and-associated-languages-codes-reference-sheet/

Even if you're using the same version of Google as a friend and input the same query, your results may not be the same. This is because Google personalises the results to you. Some of the parameters that Google uses to do this include: browsing history, location, other people's clicks for similar searches, the device you're using, past search history, and activity on other areas of Google.

There are two ways to avoid most of these issues; the first is to use In Private browsing. On Chrome that is Incognito mode, Safari - Private Window, Microsoft Edge - InPrivate and FireFox's Private Browsing. All major browsers support it so if *you have never used it before*... or cannot find yours try searching for **browser name + "private browsing"**. However, private browsing will not remove country personalisation; you have to do that manually through the Google subdomains.

Secondly, you can try signing out of Google on the computer you are using. This will help to some extent, but for the best and most consistent results we suggest using In Private browsing. Remember to clear your cache and remove your history as well.

Google Quirks

Google has a superiority complex. It thinks it knows best and, to be fair, 90% of the time it's not wrong, it shows us what we want to see. However, it will sometimes avoid or ignore your search terms in favour of others which provide a greater number of results.

Most of the time it will tell you.

Why Raking Your Leaves is Counterproductive - Return to Now
https://returntonow.net/2017/11/04/top-10-reasons-not-rake-leaves/ ▾
4 Nov 2017 - Biologists at the National Wildlife Federation are urging people to stop **raking** their **leaves**. Here's why: 1. It's unnatural. **Leaves** are meant to stay where they fall for all the reasons below. "A **leaf** layer several inches deep is a natural thing in any area where trees naturally grow," NWF says on its website.
Missing: ~~siberian desert~~

Here, we can see that 'siberian' and 'desert' are missing. However, sometimes they are not. For those of you with some experience of using quotation marks to try and guarantee inclusion of a term in the query, this is no longer 100% reliable.

So, what does Google do? It automatically looks for variations of the words used in the query, e.g. stop, stopped, stops, and stopping. It looks for synonyms (different words with the same meaning) of the words you have used. But, most importantly, you won't know the variations that Google is using. This means there will always be a little bit of black box magic with regards to how your results are shown which makes refining them a bit of a nightmare.

Exact Matches

If you want to enforce an exact match then you need to include intext:*search term.* This will make sure that the term is included in the returned results. For example, your search query may be.

plato's allegory the cave intext:counter argument

Another way to do this is to use the verbatim setting. You can access this in the search options menu after you have made a query. Click "Tools" and then "All results" to see the option to change to verbatim. This will mean that the words have to be contained in the returned results.

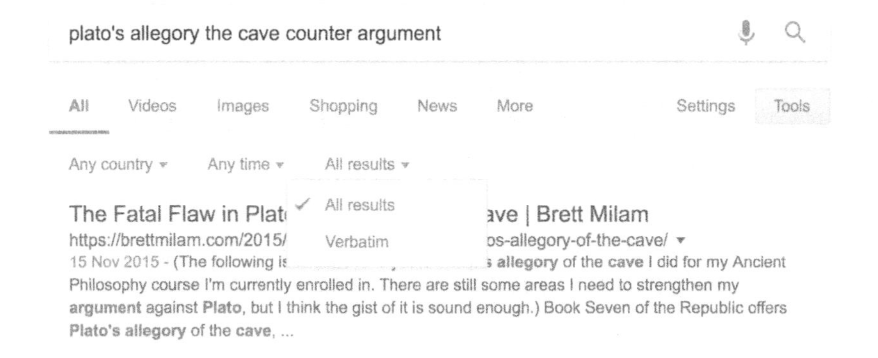

Indexing

Google has two indexes. Not everything it stores is kept in its main index; there is a supplementary index for when there are not enough results for your query. This supplementary index contains less popular, unusual and specialist material.

You cannot access it by default. Sadly, there is no simple switch to engage it. We have found that most of the time it appears to engage, as can be seen by similar queries returning different amounts (millions) of results. It appears to be used most with the verbatim search feature.

Not only do the index rankings change as time goes on, Google considers us all to be its guinea pigs and, as such, tests variations of the algorithm on us many times a year. This makes it very difficult to reproduce the exact same results if we leave significant time between queries.

- **Pro Tip**: Find a potential article or source that might help? Bookmark it. Or go one step further and create a sub folder for that specific assignment. It will make finding those resources you only briefly looked at, or looking for the appropriate reference/link if you printed it off, so much easier.

General Commands

Phrase searching

" " around phrases looks for as much of that phrase as possible, but some substitution may still occur.

"For the folly was not his, it was theirs"| 

Excluding Terms

You can use the minus sign (dash "-") to not include terms.

analysis of US presidents -Trump 

Specify Variations

You can use OR to tell Google to use a particular synonym. This will mean it won't substitute the text with its own. Sometimes, however, it is better to run separate searches.

aristotle's argument OR theory for virtue 

Any Word

The * can be used to stand in for any word, useful if you're not quite sure what you are searching for.

* windows on 18th century buildings 

In the Title

Using intitle: will confine the search of a single word to the title of documents. This is very useful if you know the name of the document or source you are looking for.

treatments for intitle:alzheimer's and dementia 

If you are looking to search for a document title then you should use allintitle: instead.

allintitle: the effects of alzheimer's disease on the family 

File Formats

It is worth thinking about file formats, especially if you've identified the resource you are looking for. Generally:

- PDFs are for research papers, industry papers, lengthy documents and government reports
- PPT and PPTX (the newer version) are PowerPoint files. There are now many different formats for presentations and different hosting services are becoming more popular, so be sure to think about different file extensions.

You can specify a file format by using filetype:format.

fire and fury filetype:pdf 

Search Websites/ Domains

When searching large websites, or groups of sites with the same base domain, you can use the 'site:' query.

asthma workplace rights site:gov.uk 

You can also combine this with the minus sign (-) in order to exclude websites.

kant's categorical imperative -site:wikipedia.com 

You can see the full list of the most commonly used operators at this address: https://support.google.com/websearch/answer/2466433

- **Pro Tip:** You can use the advance search feature to for helpful boxes to fill in rather than using query modifiers in the box - https://www.google.com/advanced_search

A Brief Word on Google Scholar

Google Scholar defines itself as providing "a simple way to broadly search for scholarly literature". And for the most part we think it is a brilliant resource. However, it has a few caveats that mean relying on it for all your research just because it's Google is not the soundest of research strategies.

1. It does not cover all key journals in all subjects.
2. Whilst Scholar will index the whole text and you may find what you are looking for, often the rest of the text is hidden behind a paywall.

- **Pro Tip:** If this is the case, try copying the title and searching Google with the query modifier for "allintitle:" and see if another website is hosting it for free.

3. It groups different versions of the same article together. So, looking for the exact article referenced by another author can be difficult.
4. Whilst it does include open access material, pre-prints, and institutional repositories, they may differ from final

published versions - charts and images may be redacted due to copyright restrictions.

5. It may not include the author archived versions on personal websites (a niche issue we admit, but one just worth mentioning).
6. There are materials on Google Scholar that are not peer-reviewed even though they appear to be structured like professional academic articles.

Technical Caveats

1. Does not use the publishers' metadata.
2. Date and author searches are in a conducted in a standard area of the document when it is scanned, so some documents that don't follow those specifications can be incorrectly dated and have the wrong author.
3. Page numbers, part of an address, or data item may be mistaken for publication year.

Google Scholar Advanced Search

If, however, you want to delve into Google Scholar and search more finely, you can use the advance search feature. Select the menu on the top left and then the "Advance Search" option to bring up the pop up.

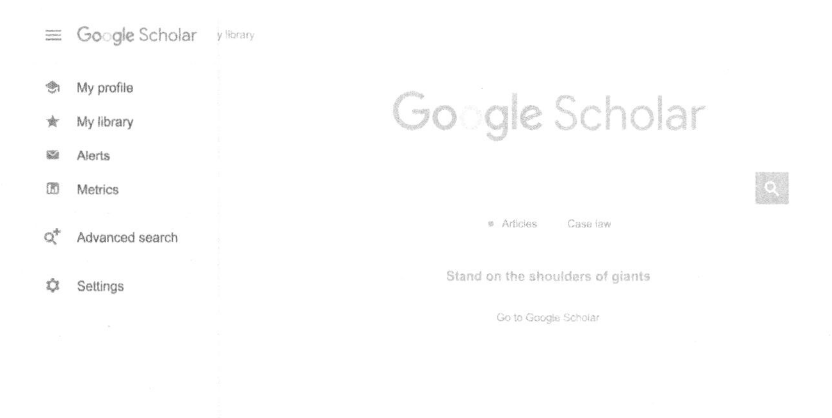

You can see search modifiers here:

https://scholar.google.com/intl/en/scholar/help.html#searching

What resources to focus on

Now you've actually found potential resources, it's time to determine which are the most useful. If you've mastered the art of speedreading then you'll be in a good place to blow through these documents. If you haven't, then it might take a little longer but you'll find it.

Finding the diamonds in the rough

When you're reading through articles, books, websites, journals, or whatever other form of research you've pinned down, it is best to have your key question in mind. The core argument of the essay can serve equally well in this situation if you are not looking to answer a specific question or the latter fails to help you focus on what you should be looking for.

With this in mind, it is helpful to take an initial look at your newly-sourced documents to rate them according to their potential contribution to your assignment. Articles directly arguing for or against one of your main points are obviously going to be more useful than those that go off at a tangent.

A scoring system works quite well here; by rating each article you can quickly prioritise those that require a more in-depth read at a later date. We don't advise spending too much time reading and trying to fully comprehend all the resources at this stage, it is better to skim and highlight potentially useful sections before rating the document.

Creating a table, where you can keep track of all your research, will help at all stages of the assignment. Here's a mock one we've created to demonstrate:

Article Name	Source	Rating	For / Against Main Thesis	1 Line Summary
Working Against the Curve	www.jstor.com/article/123msad123	7	Against	John Arthurs work on the futility of capitalism in the modern world.

If, when you are scanning through a document to determine the validity of a resource, you find something particularly useful such as a quote that directly address part of your main thesis or a piece of analysis contradictory to your main argument, then it is always worth highlighting, either virtually or with a physical highlighter, as it will save you time later.

Recommended Resources

We've compiled a list of places below that you might be able to find the resources you are looking for.

Manual

University Library

Finding things

In the old days, you may have had to use catalogue cards to find where everything was kept. Of course, now it is a little simpler. You can just use a computer - type in the book you want and its exact location will appear.

If, however, you just want to browse and see what sources are available, you can ask a librarian to direct you to the best section for a particular topic according to the **Dewey Decimal System** to get you started.

Dewey Decimal System

000 - **Generalities**

100 - **Philosophy and Psychology**

200 - **Religion**

300 - **Social Science**

400 - **Language**

500 - **Natural Science and Mathematics**

600 - **Technology (Applied Sciences)**

700 - **Arts**

800 - **Literature**

900 - **Geography and History**

Other tips

- Use your time in the library to get that initial research done. Take just a pen and some paper and discard your phone and other distractions so that you can focus on all the research or books you bought with you or found in the library.
- Bring snacks if you plan to stay a while and avoid someone stealing your seat when you get hungry.
- If you are planning on working there for a few hours, make sure you check out your university social policy on the library.... What does this mean you ask? Well, sometimes the library can be immensely popular and you'll need to get there before 8am in order to get a good seat.
- Scan the research books in the library so that only those with a high chance of being used in your essay are taken home. This reduces the chance of late fees and the strain of carrying 10+ books!

- **Pro Tip:** Some university libraries allow you to reserve books online. This can be used to your advantage if there are multiple students covering the same question or topic and there are popular or standard books on the subject.

City Libraries

Oft forgotten or relegated to last resort, depending on its size, the city library is a good alternative source of books that have either been checked out by students or are not available in your university library. It's also guaranteed to be quieter than your university library, especially around exam time or end of term essay time.

Personal Libraries

Professors normally have sky high racks of books in their offices, most of which will specific to the subjects they teach because these are topics they are currently researching or have researched in the past. Therefore, they are packed full of perfect resources that you may not even find at the university library. And there is even an expert to guide you to the right books.

Of course, the tricky part is accessing these books. Your professor may not want to part with them willingly. A one off loan here and there may be allowed but it is not a situation to be abused. After all, they are not a library, no matter how much their office may resemble one. But, most of the time, they should still be able to inform you whether or not the recommended book(s) are in the university library and, if not, what other potential sources there may be.

- **Note:** It is generally easier to borrow books if they are supervising you in a PhD/MPhil or Master's degree but, if you are an undergraduate, you may suffer from unfortunate stereotyping. In most cases, this will be unfounded but, for first years, it is probably not too far off the mark.

Online

Educational Resources Information Centre (ERIC)

Possibly one of the best resources, ERIC is maintained by the U.S. Department of Education. You'll find more than 1.3 million bibliographic records of articles and online materials on this site. The extensive body of education-related literature includes technical reports, policy papers, conference papers, research syntheses, journal articles, and books.

URL

https://eric.ed.gov/

Lexis Web

Even though it's quite niche, we figured it was it was worth mentioning the best legal research website. It populates the search engine with validated legal websites and articles.

URL

https://www.lexisweb.com/

Microsoft Academic (MA)

Microsoft Academic gives you access to 20 million publications including journals, scientific papers, and conferences. Because MA uses machine learning and a semantic search engine, it processes the natural language of its stored documents to understand and remember the relevancy and content. In theory, this provides better search results. Feel free to test for yourself.

URL

academic.research.microsoft.com/

Wolfram Alpha

Ask it a question and it returns an answer, perhaps a good way to start research on a topic you are unfamiliar with. It's not a classic 'go to' search engine but it's billed as a computational knowledge engine that computes answers rather than just giving you documents to browse.

URL

https://www.wolframalpha.com/

ResearchGate

ResearchGate is a social networking site for scientists and researchers to share papers, ask and answer questions, and find collaborators. Research Gate's collection of publications provide a vast array of works that cover timely topics including culture, the environment, politics, health, science, and space.

URL

https://www.researchgate.net/

Open Library

Find the world's classic literature, open eBooks, and other excellent open and free resources in the Open Library. It is part of the web archives initiative and has over 20 million sources!

URL

https://openlibrary.org

SpringerLink

Search through SpringerLink for electronic journals and books, it covers almost every available subject. You may need to check that your university allows you to sign in and download their content for free first though!

URL

https://link.springer.com/

Directory of Open Access Journals

The Directory of Open Access Journals is a great place for access to top-quality journal writings for free. It tends to be more scientific in nature but it is a great place to investigate.

URL

https://doaj.org/

Jstor

A great, general host of journals, books and other materials that can be used for your essay. As a general rule, most universities provide all students with free access to this site.

URL

https://www.jstor.org/

Guttenburg

Free books that have expired copyright - great for the English student.

URL

https://www.gutenberg.org/

Kopernio

Last but certainly not least, this little gem of an extension is a new thing on the market that helps students get past paywalls for articles... That's right, it finds you free versions of that article on the web. If your university library doesn't have access then this is definitely the next best option. You install it as a plugin on Chrome and it finds free versions of those pesky journals that you need. *It was in Alpha when we tested it, so it may be even better now!*

URL

https://kopernio.com/

CHAPTER FOUR: NOTE-TAKING

Introduction

After you've assembled a stack of papers and books or created a folder full of pdfs of journal papers, all of hopefully sound quality, and perhaps assembled a good index of all the research you've done, ranking the sources on their potential usefulness, you're ready to pick up pen and paper and begin searching for the information you need.

In this section, we'll cover the different types of notes you might make, branching out past research notes to include some information on taking notes in lectures and using them for exams. On that slight detour, we'll take a look at the science of memory and things you can do to improve your recall. We will also show you how to condense your notes and turn key words into triggers to help with those essays you have to write in exams.

There will be information on the different systems of note-taking, that's right, there are systems and some are more effective than others. Plus, we'll give you a breakdown of some of the most popular tech available to assist you.

Purpose

The most important thing to ask yourself before you start taking notes is...

"What is the purpose of your notes?"

Are you aiming to condense information from a journal? Are you listing out potentially useful quotes? Are you trying to create relationships between different sources? Are you putting together an argument? Are you trying to solve the answer to a question?

Knowing the purpose of your notes help you organise how you are going to take them and what information you are looking for. It helps your brain shift through all the fluff to find the golden nuggets that you need. If you just set out absent-mindedly, you'll find yourself just reproducing the content in front of you - whatever that may be.

Type

It is best to start with the type of notes you are going to take. This will help you decide on their purpose later.

Lecture

Lecture notes are a notoriously difficult subject. Lectures vary in quality, content and style... all the time. Therefore, the best methods for creating lecture notes will also vary. However, there are a few general things about lecture notes that we have identified.

- **Timing is everything.** During a lecture, there is only so much time devoted to each slide or point and the lecturer will rarely pause and wait for you to catch up. Therefore, deciding how much information you want to capture is undeniably important.
- **Try and isolate the large overarching concepts of the lecture.** The main point that the lecturer is trying to make. Jot these down and then, either during or straight after the lecture, add some of the extra information that helps connect the dots to how these larger ideas are formed.

- **Supplementary information is also key.** These are the little titbits mentioned that are not contained on the slides. If you are lucky, your lectures may be recorded making it easier to find these later, however, if they are not, then you'll be stuck with only the slides from the lecture. Therefore, it is always a good idea to make a note of the interesting supplementary information especially if it links to authors or books relating to the subject.
- If you don't get automatic access to the slides after the lecture, make sure to ask for them as they will reduce the amount of work you have to do to make notes.
- Illustrating how information connects to each other, through diagrams is a useful tactic to reinforce your understanding after the lecture.
- A good lecture will pose questions that spur you to find the answers; it will try and capture your intrigue. If you have questions about the topic, write them down and make them easy to find by pairing them with symbols (see below).

Essay

Essay notes differ from lecture notes in one key way - the time restriction is lifted. The only time constraints are self-inflicted;

if you choose to write your essays the night before, that's your choice - we wish you luck. Again, we've put together some general tips for essay notes, otherwise known as research notes.

- This style is generally hyper-specific, you are looking for certain information and that's it, the rest can readily be discarded. This means some sources will have notes going on for days as they contain tonnes of highly relevant information. Others will have only one quote on them.
- Use a separate page/file/document or whatever you need to separate your notes. Having them all on the same page not clearly titled or labelled will make it a nightmare when trying to track information down at a later date.
- Draw links between key ideas and thoughts, if different authors are sprouting a similar or contradictory analysis, note down their possible 'partner' and where you've made notes to make your life easier later.
- You should have an idea in your head about what sort of information you're looking for where, whether this is arguments, counter arguments, initial points or evidence etc. You can mark notes with symbols or

highlight them a different colour depending on what they are. For example:

POINT OF INTEREST	SYMBOL	COLOUR
EVIDENCE	(E)	ORANGE
ARGUMENT	(A)	GREEN
COUNTER ARGUMENT	(CA)	GREEN
QUOTE	(Q)	BLUE
EXAMPLE	(EX)	ORANGE
ALTERNATIVE VIEW	(AV)	YELLOW
SOLUTION	(S)	GREEN
REFERENCE	(R)	BLUE

(These could be any symbols and any colours, just thought we'd get you started.)

Revision (Exams)

Most people revise for exams by making notes. They have a series of revision materials, or the original course/subject materials, and they meticulously go through creating notes for things they need to learn. We're not going to tell people to change those methods that work for them. That being said, there are tactics you can use to drastically increase your retention rates. We'll be looking at these in the memory section. For now, here are some general tips on creating revision notes:

- **Split your notes into facts and ideas.** This way you can start attributing facts with ideas and pairing them in your head for a better chance of recalling them in the exam.
- **Decide on the level of depth needed for each topic.** For example, if you have to answer three essay questions in as many hours then you'll only have an hour for each one. How much can you feasibly write in an hour? This should help you decide the quantity of notes you need.
- **Look for the trade-offs.** Ask your professor for the format. If there are six topics in the course and six questions - then there will most likely be one question on each topic (but it's worth checking). If you only have to answer one question then you can prepare one topic in depth, so you know it like the back of your hand, and then have a backup topic in case the question on your main topic is horrific. This reduces the number of notes you have to make and memorise.

What is better – hand-written notes or typed?

In short:

Hand writing is for input.

Typing is for output.

In long:

The science behind this recommendation is that writing notes by hand forces you to synthesise the information, which helps you remember and recall it. When we take notes by hand, we generally can't keep pace with the information coming in, thus our brains respond by categorising it into important ("write this down") and unimportant ("can skip that"). This distinction is important in the brain; it assists in marking the information we've classified as important and, when we are forced to classify information, it becomes 'stickier' in our heads.

Typing, however, comes into its own when we want to reduce the lag between thought and writing down. This is called transcription fluency. The faster you can get your thoughts on paper or screen the better. This is why words typed out are less likely to be forgotten or lost in the process. Therefore, the faster and quicker you can type, the easier it will be to communicate your ideas and arguments.

So, to reiterate - if you want to remember information, write it by hand. However, if you want to communicate information, then it is better to type.

Of course, this technical analysis doesn't account for preference or the ability to reorganise and reproduce typed notes. Typing speed may also be a factor if you find yourself needing a large quantity of notes in a short amount of time and there isn't an immediate requirement to be able to remember the contents.

Systems of Note-taking

As you are about to see, there are several different systems for taking notes. We've included some of the most popular below and talked about their pros and cons. Using a system to take notes can be particularly effective. It keeps them organised and structured, making it easier to find what you're looking for later and allowing your brain to create structured relationships between thoughts.

The Sentence Method

SENTENCE METHOD

(1) **Define a Topic**
Make sure when defining a topic, it is not too large.

(2) **Condense point**
Take the point that the teacher, lecturer or book is trying to make and summarise it.

(3) **Write sentence**
Take the mental summary and write it out as a single sentence under the topic heading.

(4) **Repeat**
Do this for each topic covered.

TOPIC
Sentence describing a key point in the topic.
Sentence describing a key point in the topic.
Sentence describing a key point in the topic.
Sentence describing a key point in the topic.
Sentence describing a key point in the topic.
TOPIC
Sentence describing a key point in the topic.
Sentence describing a key point in the topic.
Sentence describing a key point in the topic.
Sentence describing a key point in the topic.
Sentence describing a key point in the topic.
Sentence describing a key point in the topic.
Sentence describing a key point in the topic.
TOPIC
Sentence describing a key point in the topic.
Sentence describing a key point in the topic.
Sentence describing a key point in the topic.
Sentence describing a key point in the topic.
Sentence describing a key point in the topic.
Sentence describing a key point in the topic.

BEST FOR:
LECTURES

The Sentence Method is perhaps the simplest system. It is probably also going to be closest to how you take notes at the moment - a large list of sentences, phrases or facts condensed categorised underneath topics. The difference is that it places emphasis on condensing points down and writing them in your own words rather than copying verbatim. This increases the chance of you memorising and understanding the content.

PROS:

- Quick to implement and use
- Reduces the amount of information you need to capture
- Can help with later reviewing
- Ideal when you want a simple method of note-taking

CONS:

- Little better than listing out the original content
- Doesn't assist in building relationships between content
- Makes it hard to supplement your written topics later

Mind Map Methods

MIND MAPPING

① **Central idea**
What is the main topic or subject of your notes? Place this in the center of your page.

② **Subtopics**
Subtopics should circle the main idea, branching off like a tree.

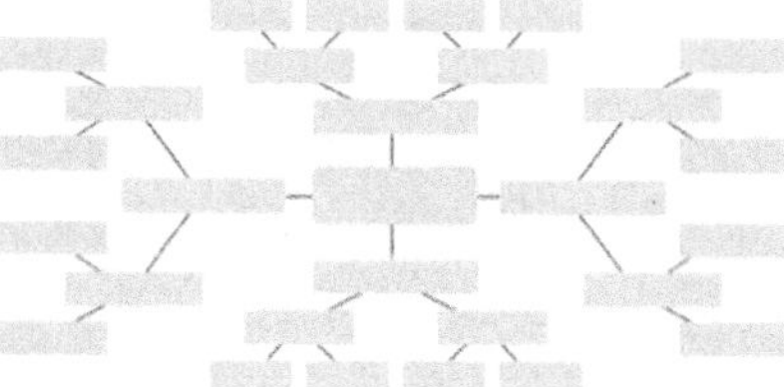

③ **Key Information**
Branching out from sub-topics should be all the key information (facts, dates, short explanations).

④ **Connecting the dots**
You can extend these branches out as far as the page will allow. It is also a good idea to illustrate how they connect to each other, using different colours to show relationships links.

BEST FOR:

VISUAL LEARNERS

The Mind Mapping method is perfect for those who need to see relationships between ideas. It also serves those who like to take their time and illustrate their thought processes. You can really break topics down with a mind map, spreading them out into important clusters of information before adding in lines to connect similar or contrasting ideas. It really allows you to express creativity in your note-taking.

PROS:

- Easily visualise difficult topics
- Actively understand how things tie together
- Improve your memory of the topic by having a physical image to remember rather than blocks of text

CONS:

- Takes a lot of time to do
- Not suited to taking notes quickly
- Can get distracted by the creation aspect over the learning aspect

Outlining Method

OUTLINING METHOD

① **Main Topic**
Title the page with the main topic

② **Subtopics**
Every time there is a new subtopic indent slightly and write it down.

③ **Key Information**
Under each subtopic, keeping it short and sweet, write down the key points and facts that make up that subtopic.

MAIN TOPIC
Subtopic
- Key point
- Key point
- Key point
- Key fact

Subtopic
- Key fact
- Key point
- Key point
- Key fact
- Key fact
- Key fact

Subtopic
- Key point
- Key fact
- Key point
- Key point

BEST FOR:
KEY INFORMATION

The Outlining Method is a more focused version of the Sentence Method. Instead of just summarising points, you are looking to pull out key information and facts and breaking down main topics in to subtopics to better organise your notes. This is a super quick method that works well for certain subjects, resources or lectures.

PROS:

- Very quick
- Minimal writing needed
- Well organised
- Easy to find key facts and information

CONS:

- Not very detailed
- Some facts and their relevance may be lost
- Only works well with certain types of information

Charting Methods

CHARTING METHOD

MAIN TOPIC

Subtopic	Subtopic	Subtopic
Key fact	Key fact	Key fact
Key fact	Key fact	Key fact
Key fact	Key fact	Key fact
Key fact	Key fact	Key fact
	Key fact	Key fact
	Key fact	Key fact
	Key fact	

Subtopic	Subtopic
Key fact	Key fact
Key fact	Key fact
Key fact	Key fact
Key fact	Key fact
	Key fact

1. **Main Topic**
   Title the page with the main topic
2. **Split into columns**
   For every new subtopic you should create another column. If you want wider columns or more subtopics then you can split the page in half.
3. **Subtopics**
   Title each column with subtopics that run underneath the main topic.
4. **Key facts**
   Using the charting methods works best for storying small facts of figures, rather than complicated and long explanations.

BEST FOR:

FACTS

The Charting Method is again one that focuses on key facts. Very similar to the Outlining and Sentence Methods, it works by splitting your notes into columns, reducing the amount you can store in each. By doing this it makes sure only the most important aspects are recorded. Further, you can easily go back to other subtopics and add more information as you go along, making the notes more concise and well ordered.

PROS:

- Very well organised
- Easily allows information to be placed in relevant subtopics
- Makes finding facts easy across multiple subtopics

CONS:

- Only works well with small pieces of information
- May get confusing if you're not used to splitting main topics into subtopics
- Takes some time getting used to the non-linear note taking

Cornell Method

CORNELL METHOD

Key Notes | Notes

Summary

1. **Divide page**
   Using a ruler or going free hand, divide the page into 3 sections as we've shown to the left.
2. **Simple notes**
   During your lecture, or whilst reading through the resource, use this column to make simple notes. These are building blocks of your notes.
3. **Multiple sheets**
   You can fill up as many sheets as you need to adequately cover the topic.
4. **Key notes**
   After you've finished taking notes, go back through each sheet and summarise the simple notes in 1-3 key points.
5. **Relationships/ Summary**
   Once you've summarised all the key notes, then it's time to compare them to the rest of the key notes you've taken, writing down relationships and/or summaries in this bottom section.

BEST FOR:

EVERYTHING

The Cornell Method was designed by Walter Pauk in the 1940s at Cornell University and we believe is the best method for taking notes across the board. This is because it allows you to take fuller, more detailed notes before condensing them to key facts and producing a summary.

PROS:

- Covers all the key note taking practises
- Offers the opportunity for note reviewing
- Allows large information chunks to be collected
- Forces the note-taker to think about how things link together for the summary/relationship section

CONS:

- Requires additional work, after taking the original notes, to be most effective

➢ **Pro Tip:** When revising, take all the sheets for one subject and lay them out so that only the key information section is shown. You can then test your understanding of the key concepts and easily identify what you've missed, thus reducing the time needed to make notes. Your revision notes are ready at the first hurdle.

Taking Notes on a Computer

All of these methods can be replicated on a computer. There is no requirement to use a pen and paper. However, there are some benefits with the latter, for example, increasing the quantity of information you absorb and store in your memory and lessening the possibility of distraction.

If you are planning to take notes on a computer, there are many pieces of software that can help. You can also simply get away with a text editor on your computer (every computer has one) or use a free word processor like Google Docs.

If you want to look at more unique software, check out our recommendations at the end of the chapter. These include specific mind-mapping software and programs designed to assist you in note-taking.

Other Note-Taking Solutions

Beyond taking notes by hand or by computer, you can also use digital recorders, voice-to-text, auto-note compilers, and other people's notes.

Digital recorders

Ever seen a character in a film speaking into a little device, talking to it and telling it to do whatever? Louis, in the TV series *Suits,* has one that he uses occasionally. Anyway, these are digital recorders, or microphone recorders. You speak into them and then play back what you said at a later date.

A digital recorder may be useful if you find it easier not to interrupt your train of thought to write things down. Or if your thoughts are a little too rambling in nature to write down, speaking out loud may help to clarify them.

Journalists have been using recording devices for years, long before they became so small and easy to carry around. How else would they be able to interview people and give them their full attention? Having some way of recording responses to questions allows journalists to type up the notes later.

Voice to Text

Every year, voice recognition technology gets better and better. Computers are vastly improving their understanding of the nuances of human speech and converting it into text. If you are someone who has trouble typing, you may already interact with your computer via voice commands.

The benefits of using your voice to record notes are clear:

- Reduces the time and effort of typing them out
- Allows you to read and take notes at the same time
- Makes copying quotes less laborious
- Generally, a far faster process

The old downside of having to spend half as much time again going back over the notes to correct miss-written words or weird half-formed words is slowly disappearing.

There are specific text to speech software packages available. Companies have been working on the problem for years and now have fully-formed, high functioning products. And then there are the more recent developments that use machine learning to improve their reliability. We've outlined the best options in the software section below.

If you don't have the budget to buy software or simply want to try out voice to text options before you commit, we suggest using the voice to text converter on your smartphone. Most iPhones and Android phones have this feature already built in. You can access it with the microphone button on your keyboard.

(iPhone example)

Some services allow you to upload audio files of you speaking and then try to turn them into text. These have varying results but are likely to get better with time. If you really, really don't want to type out your own voice notes, it is possible to get other people to do it. There are sites that specialise in transcribing services.

- **Pro Tip:** If you have dyslexia you should be entitled to this type of software through your university. Talk to disability support and see if they can get it for you.

Auto Note Compilers

Now, these aren't as good as they could be. There is still a long way to go from being able to upload a research paper or PowerPoint document and have a machine create beautiful notes for you. But it is probably not that far off.

There are auto summary generators online that take text and keep only the most relevant parts. This can severely reduce your workload; if you have 100,000 words to go through, you can condense it to around 10% of its original mass.

Their reliability is obviously occasionally dubious. So, we would not recommend this approach unless you have a good understanding of the topic already. However, in a pinch, they can provide the acceleration needed in order to get those projects completed and handed in.

- **Something to watch for:** Still in its early stages, Cram101 is an AI that condenses textbooks into notes and summaries and also creates theoretically unlimited flashcards and true or false answer questions from the original text allowing you to test yourself. There is real opportunity in the years to come for this technology to be advanced and improved upon.

Other People's work

Last, but not least, you can always ask your friends if they wouldn't mind sharing their notes. This is, of course, going to vary in response from friend to friend, and you may need a good excuse as to why you haven't created any of your own. Or look for something to trade in return. Or, if they are super nice people, then you might just get away with it... the first time. However, the more you ask, the less likely they are to keep giving without receiving something in return.

You could formalise this approach by creating a group of people that all go to the same lectures but assign one person to take notes at each lecture in turn. They then share their notes with the group and don't have to do it again until their turn comes around again. This create a mutual benefit for all.

Watch out for those people who don't do it when it is their turn, however, as they will throw the entire system into jeopardy. It is recommended that you only do this with small numbers of people that you trust to not only take the notes but also put in the effort level required. The larger the group, the less likely you are to have that level of trust and a mutual upholding of the agreement.

How to improve your note-taking and takeaways:

During our time at University and through conversations with other students we've come up with some sure-fire ways to improve your note-taking abilities and also improve what you get out of them.

1. Touch Typing

Now, in this day and age, touch typing may not be something we need to stress as an important skill amongst the student population. However, there is always room for improvement. One of the things that makes touch typing so effective is that you don't need to look at the keyboard. You can imagine how handy this is when you are in lectures - you can pay attention to the slides and the professors whilst your hands dance on the keyboard. Or, if you have a document open on one side of the screen and a word processor on the other, you can easily read and take notes at the same time.

It is considered good enough in the workplace to type at 40 words per minute (wpm). However, if you really want to see a marked improvement in the amount of content you can capture in a short space of time we'd suggest aiming to double that speed. If you can achieve over 100 wpm consistently, then you'll be in the same class as people that type professionally for a living.

A few years ago, learning to touch type was a pain. It involved gruelling self-practise and basically just reading and typing at the same time. Thankfully, some intrepid web developers have come up with different games, exercises and competitions that really make the process significantly easier to learn.

One that we would recommend is https://www.typingclub.com - it has a series of exercises and practise motivators plus it is beautifully designed. Of course, nothing but practice is really going to help you improve so you'll have to try and work daily if you want to see real improvements.

If you're the competitive type, and already have a reasonable typing speed (70+ wpm) we recommend checking out http://play.typeracer.com/. This website lets you race against people around the world or you can send a direct link to your friends and race them.

2. Recording your notes

Following on from the digital recorder section earlier, once you have compiled your notes, it may help you with recall and learning to record them through a microphone. It can be the one on your computer, the one on your phone or a specialised one. Whatever microphone it is, it doesn't really matter; all you want to do is make sure that the recording is clearly named and confirmed at the start of the recording to verify that you're listening to the right information.

Once you start recording, you need to speak clearly and relatively slowly, making sure you leave appropriate pauses in between new topics or subtopics. Once you have gone through a main topic and all the notes, stop the recording, label it and store it. Then do the same for the other main topics. You can decide how you want to split up your notes and how long you want the recordings to be before you start.

Once you have all the recordings, you can then start listening to them whenever you have time. You can play them back whilst you go about your chores, for example, and help cement them in your memory. If you want to double down on reinforcement, then we suggest listening while reading your original notes.

For those of you who cannot stand the sound of your own voice, you have a couple of options. 1) Find someone else that has the same problem and swap with them; you record their notes and they record yours. 2) Ask your house-mate or friend to do it for you. This, of course, relies on them being willing to spend a few hours recording notes for you. Introducing them to the technique may end up making them want to try it for themselves and then you're potentially back to the first solution. 3) There are text-to-voice synthesisers on the web that you can upload the text to and they speak it to you. If you use the free versions, the voice is likely to sound like a robot.

VOICE RECORDINGS

1
Create your notes, taking care to make them legible

2
Find a method to record your voice

3
Split your notes into main topics for each recording

4
Record those notes, one main topic at a time

5
Label your recordings accurately

6
Listen to your recordings often to improve recall

3. Virtual Paper (iPad Style)

One way that can drastically improve your ability to keep track of notes and make them organised is using a tablet. But only a good tablet. Unfortunately, there are many cheap tablets that are great for watching the occasional film and browsing the web. However, beyond word processing as note taking, which is not what we are referring to, they aren't best suited to improving your notes.

However, there are a few tablets out there where, at least on some level, some serious thought has gone into this. They allow you to treat the screen as if it were a piece of paper. There is no dodgy misinterpretation of your palm on the screen, no delay as the pencil slides long the glass and the line is drawn behind.

Using this kind of tablet is like writing on paper, but with all the benefits of a digital product. You can undo rather than cross out. You can take your organisation to the next level: drag and drop photos or images, directly annotate slides from the lecture (whilst in the lecture) and add audio snippets to different sections. Plus, you have the added bonus of handwriting your notes, which, as we've already mentioned, improves retention of your notes.

You can check out the tablets that we would recommend below. Unfortunately, this kind of tech doesn't come cheap currently. We have found using a cheaper tablet to do this results in an experience that is more aggravating than rewarding as they tend to hinder rather than help.

4. Shorthand

Perhaps you just want to use pen and paper? This is a viable option, especially, if you improve your speed of note taking by learning shorthand. We're going to give you a quick guide on how to learn this skill.

Background

There are many forms of shorthand and many different systems. Some working on symbols rather than letters, others using phonetics and some by cutting down the amount of content you have to write.

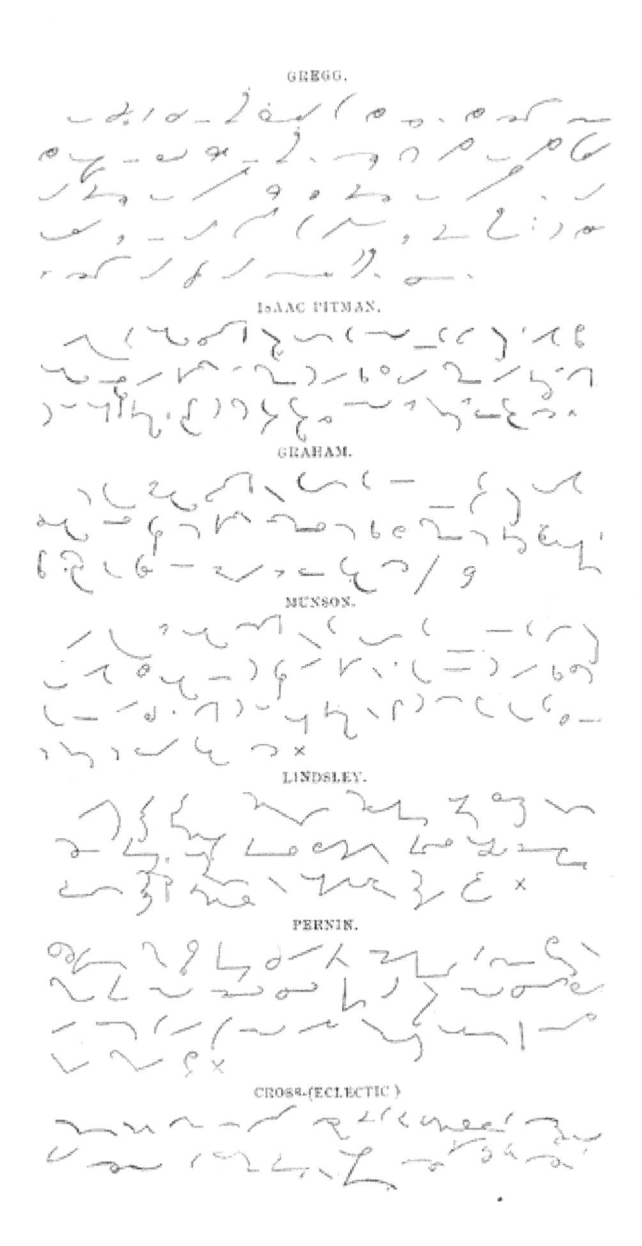

Above is a series of examples of different forms. Looks incomprehensible, right? Well, that is true, certain forms make it so you have to learn how to read and write again. However, our favourite is a version that lessens the need to learn a series of new symbols and instead focuses on reducing the number of words that you need to write. Wielded properly, these tools can let people write up to and exceeding 100 wpm. This is insane considering the average person writes at around 15-20 wpm.

But let's get to it, how can you start to achieve these five-fold increases?

Teeline Shorthand

The shorthand we have chosen is called Teeline. It is widely regarded as one of the easiest to learn and the results are equal to some of the more complicated systems. Alastair Campbell used Teeline to write his dairies when he was serving as Tony Blair's spokesman. At its core, it works by removing unnecessary letters and making the letters themselves quicker to write.

Basics

1. **Omit silent letters:**
    - bake becomes bak (the silent e at the end is omitted)
    - crumb becomes crum (the final b is silent)
    - wedge becomes weg (the d is incorporated in the g sound)
    - hatch becomes hch (the t is incorporated in the ch sound)
    - might becomes mit (the gh is silent)
2. **Omit vowels in the middle of words:**
    - make -> mak becomes mk
    - dumb -> dum becomes dm
    - hedge -> heg becomes hg

- know becomes nw (although silent, the W, here, is always necessary)
- girl becomes grl (although silent, the R, here, is always necessary)

IMPORTANT:

Vowels at the start of a word and those whose sound is required for the end are not removed. For example, 'about' is written abt, and 'cafe' is written cfe.

3. **Omit one of double letters or sounds:**
    - spliff becomes splf, bill becomes bl
    - luck becomes lc (c and k have the same sound thus counting as a double letter)

IMPORTANT:

Use c for 'ck', 'k' for words ending 'ke'.

4. **Use the phonetic versions of consonant combinations like 'gh' and 'ph'**
    - trough becomes trf
    - laugh becomes lf
    - telephone becomes tlfn

Using these techniques reduce words to what are called outlines. These outlines can sometimes have multiple meanings i.e. book -> bk and bike -> bk. But, generally, context will provide the correct interpretation.

Adjusting your handwriting

Once you have understood how to condense words into their outlines it is time to learn how to modify the alphabet to increase speed of writing.

TEELINE ALPHABET

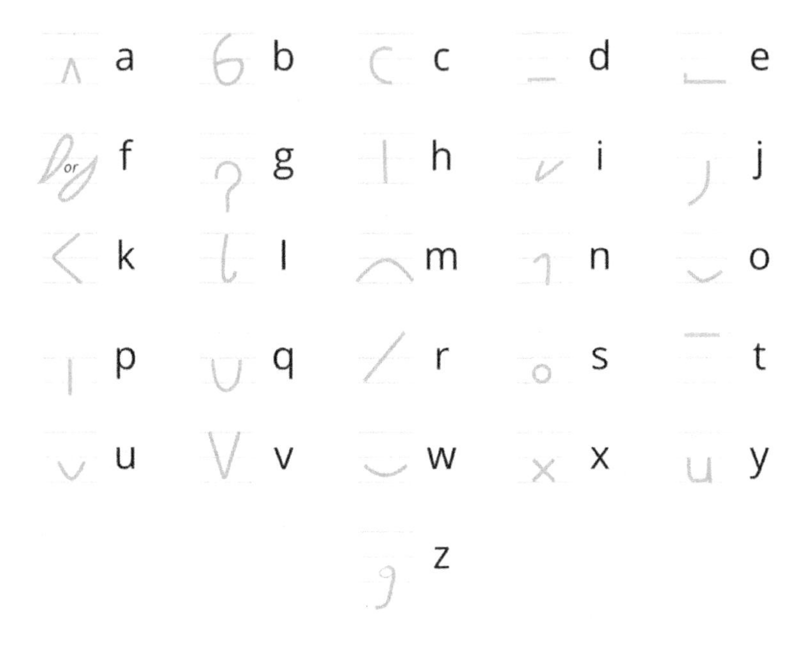

Above is the Teeline Alphabet, it looks weird, doesn't it? Slightly familiar with some absolute curve balls mixed in. This is because it is fast to write. The letters are meant to flow together in ways they don't in the normal alphabet.

Start out by writing some of these words in their outline form:

light -> lt

bear -> br

edge -> eg

tough -> tf

Once you've done that, see if you can't do it again, but this time picking other outlines and seeing if you can join the letters together. Not all letters go together but most of them do in some way. Primarily, the goal is to avoid taking the pen off the paper and write in one continuous stroke. Check out the examples below if you need some inspiration. Whilst there are 'correct' ways to join a lot of letters, most of them are intuitive. If you stop thinking about writing solely in a left to right manner, and work with the idea that you can do things vertically, and that the pen shouldn't leave the page, you will get the hang of it far quicker.

TEELINE CONNECTED EXAMPLES

Written	Word	Outline	Explanation
	duck	DC	*The 'C' hangs downwards from the 'D'.*
	back	BC	*The 'C' appears to be behind the 'B' however reading top through bottom shows clearly which was written first, 'C' is also representing 'CK' here.*
	cake	CK	*Both the 'C' and the 'K' join nicely here as they are roughly the same size.*
	food	FD	*It is best to use the upward loop when an 'F' precedes a 'D' as this allows an easy join at the end of the downstroke and anchors the it to the bottom line.*
	match	MCH	*Because 'M' is horizontal it can be used like a small letter and raised up to allowing the following letter to stand in the correct position.*

Of course, you may want to indicate an end of a sentence or a new paragraph so here are the simple and quick ways to incorporate some grammar in Teeline.

Of course, writing Teeline will get easier over time, the more you practise the easier it becomes. We recommend just writing the outlines of words first in the standard alphabet to figure out how to condense words down to only a few letters. Then you can work on incorporating the new style of alphabet into your notes

TEELINE GRAMMAR

/ Full stop // Paragraph ⟵⟶ Dash

Obviously, this isn't a complete guide, in fact there are books several times longer than this one that go into the finer art of how to use Teeline. If you would like to learn more, we suggest either buying another book or checking out YouTube.

Memorising those notes

Not all essays you'll write will have the benefit of open books next or easy access to notes. You may have to write essays in exam halls, trying your best to scrawl out as many coherent words as possible. To do this to the best of your ability you will need to have a solid plan for memorising your notes and your essay plans. In this section, we'll briefly cover some techniques that you can use to improve your recall.

Effective Notes

The best way to memorise your notes is to organise, to repeat, and to condense. These three steps will help you store the information and make it easier to recall. The process starts with the original material. Whether it be books, websites, journals or other resources, the material is read and condensed into your first set of notes. If you have an exam with multiple questions or topics, you will need to cover enough breadth to allow you to answer pretty much any question that comes up. In order to do this, you are going to have a lot of notes.

Once you have your full notes, covering everything you think you'll need, read over the notes with a highlighter or a red pen perhaps to underline the most important points: definitions, dates, facts, equations, formulae, important quotes, highly relevant authors/commentators and potentially other things. Then, take all that you've underlined or highlighted and condensed it onto a few sheets of paper.

Manually doing this, writing it out rather than copying and pasting on a computer, will significantly increase the amount you retain. Remember to read over all that you have written so far. Repetition is key to ingraining facts.

EXAM/ REVISION NOTES

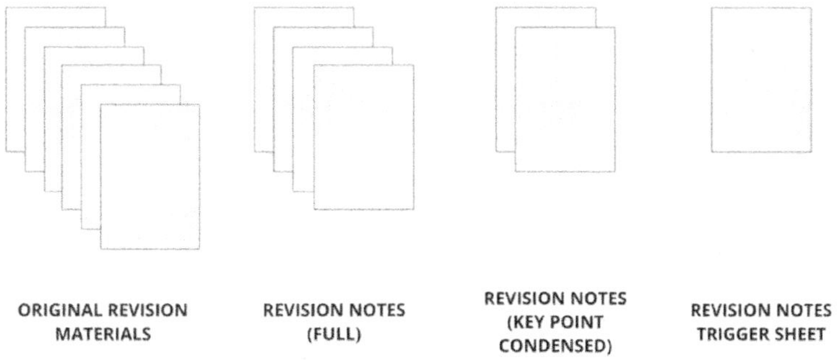

ORIGINAL REVISION MATERIALS

REVISION NOTES (FULL)

REVISION NOTES (KEY POINT CONDENSED)

REVISION NOTES TRIGGER SHEET

Once you have condensed the notes to all the key points for each topic it is time to build a trigger sheet for each exam. A trigger sheet is sadly not as exciting as it sounds. It's basically a super condensed version of your 'key point' notes - with a starter trigger word, date or author. It is important that the trigger word does its best to encapsulate as much of the concept as possible. Your goal is to be able to fit all the information in this condensed form on one side of lined A4 (although if you have slightly thicker lined paper, you may use 2 sides).

TRIGGER NOTES

Topic Title	
Trigger word	Short key phrases, describing the concept, in your own words, trying to keep it to a maximum of two lines
Author	Relevant quote that exemplifies a key point or short key phrase description of their argument/position
Date	What happened on that date

Using these sets of notes, you can now start committing them to memory. Read through your 'key point' notes and then fold the trigger notes down along the line you have drawn, leaving only the trigger words visible. Then, without looking at the descriptions, start talking out loud (this is key, actually speaking not only helps you remember, but it prevents you from 'claiming' to know without actually putting it into words).

Try and remember everything you can about that specific trigger word and what it links to. At this stage, the aim is not to remember what you've written specifically but as much of what you've written as you can. If nothing comes to mind for that trigger word, mark it and move on. Once you've gone all the way through them once, take a well-deserved break.

For all those trigger words that you couldn't remember anything about, go back to the 'key point' notes and review them again. Those that you could speak about, check the trigger information to see what you missed. If you feel like you missed a lot for certain words, treat them like you didn't know and review the 'key point' notes. The intention here is to reinforce your weakest areas so you maintain a good level of knowledge about the whole topic rather than just reinforcing what you already know. Repeating this cycle over and over will result in the slow build-up of the information in your brain.

Make a Story or a Palace

One way to memorise the trigger words is to make a story with them. Humans thrive off stories, our brains are wired to respond, memorise and recall stories better than anything else. It doesn't have to be one long story containing all the triggers, it can be a series of short stories.

For example, let's say five of your trigger words are - *Aristotle, Identity, Time, Ship and Clone.*

*A space**ship** named **Aristotle** landed on **time** thanks to its **clone** pilots, even though they were arguing over the **identity** of the stowaway.*

Far more memorable than a simple list. Obviously, these can be as complicated, as extreme or as silly as you want them to be. In fact, the more extreme or stupid they are, the easier they are to remember. When you get to the exam, you can recount these stories and trigger the related concepts.

If you find this concept difficult to achieve then you can always try another system. Made famous by Benedict Cumberbatch, in Sherlock, the mind palace is a real memory enhancing technique, although the method varies slightly from the one used on the show. Instead of creating your own imaginary palace, it is best to take a place you know really well. Somewhere like your childhood home, or your grandparents' house. A place where you've spent countless hours and can walk through in your mind.

Then you need to imagine yourself starting at the front door, what's on the front door? A piece of paper and on that piece of paper is a trigger word and what it is supposed to trigger. Stepping inside you see a hallway, on the wall is a second trigger word, before reaching a hall table where a third greets you.

See how this goes? You can find as many places to store these virtual notes as possible. Take your time and really solidify them in your mind. Running over them repetitively will reinforce them into your memory. This method is particularly helpful if you need to remember the steps for a formula, or a series of dates, as you can assign rooms to different things. Say the living room is the events that led up to World War 1, or a bedroom is an equation for rotation.

Tools

As promised we have broken down a list of all the tools that can assist you in this part of the essay writing process.

Devices

iPad Pro & Apple Pencil

The iPad pro and the Apple Pencil together are a dynamite combo. As we mentioned earlier, unless you have a good product there is no substitute for pen and paper really. The palm rejection with this device is the best we've found. As for software, there are several apps that you can use to take notes: we would recommend - **Goodnotes 4, Notability and Penultimate.**

ReMarkable E-Ink Tablet

The ReMarkable tablet is cheaper than an iPad pro and has a more focused purpose. It is designed to be both an e-reader and notebook. You can sketch and take notes, but also mark-up e-books or documents. Its palm rejection is strong and works well. The major benefit over the iPad pro is the price, however, it cannot be used as a complete computer replacement thus reducing its ability to be your one stop device.

Microsoft Surface Book 2 & Surface Pro 4

The last devices on our list are more all in one systems. If you're a fan of the Windows operating system then these may be more in line with your preference. Again, they are on the expensive side, however, they have similar levels of note taking ability as the iPad Pro and the added bonus of being a fully loaded computer. The **Surface Book 2,** in particular, can run high end software which, if you require for your course, may make it worth it on its own.

Mind Mapping Software

Mind mapping can really help some people; they find it their preferred method for taking notes and visualising things. Using software can help speed up the process and makes editing far easier. However, we completely understand if there is no substitute for a piece of A3 paper and a bunch of coloured pens.

As with all software, trying before buying is key to understanding whether it will help you.

Bubbl.us

This is an online web-based service, meaning you can access from any computer at any time. They have a free tier which allows you to make three mind maps and a paid tier which unlocks everything.

URL

https://bubbl.us/

Coggle

This is a Chrome extension; therefore, it works in your

browser. There are three variations – one is free and two are paid. When looking at simplicity and power, it is an effective tool with many good features. For example, no image limits, supports coloured branches, and supports MarkDown (a simple way to format documents on the fly). It also has version tracking so you can see who changed what.

URL

https://coggle.it/

SketchBoard

Whilst SketchBoard is not necessarily touted solely as a mind mapping tool, its collaborative white boarding features make it particularly useful for group work. However, a whiteboard is a good-a-place as any to make mind maps, even on your own, and when working on group project this tool might be a life-saver.

URL

https://sketchboard.io/

Draw.io

Advertised more as a flow chart creator than a mind mapper, Draw has a few unique and useful features. For example, it integrates with Google Drive meaning that everything you do can be stored in your Google account for easy access later. It is also free to use and delivers a simple, intuitive user interface.

URL

https://www.draw.io/

Text-to-voice software

These are tools that will speak to you, bring your notes to life, take that journal article and allow you to sit there and make notes with pen and paper as it is read to you in a synthetic voice.

Word Talk

Developed by the University of Edinburgh, this tool is a plug-in for your word processor (Word) and provides a simple text to voice function allowing it to read back to your essay (good for editing), or your notes if you want to learn them. Plus, it is completely free!

URL

http://www.wordtalk.org.uk/home/

Natural Readers

Possibly the best text-to-voice solution, natural readers is a series of beautifully designed products that provide a good service. Whilst their commercial version and pro-version are a little expensive, the free web-based version should be good enough for most people. You can drag and drop files of most standard formats and they will work easily and quickly.

URL

https://www.naturalreaders.com/

Voice-to-Text Software

Whilst most computer systems have a form of dictation now, we aren't going to go deeper into the Apple version that we have already mentioned, but there is also a Window's version – both of these come free with the Operating System on your device (modern devices).

Google Doc's Voice Typing

Completely free and brilliantly accurate, this tool is perhaps the easiest and quickest to get going, especially if you have a google account already. We find that it gets one or two words wrong in every 500 which, considering you don't have to sound like a robot when talking, is a great plus. We'd suggest learning the voice commands to make your life even more hands free. Voice typing works in 43 languages but only English for editing and formatting.

URL

https://docs.google.com

Dragon Naturally Speaking

Nuance's DNS technology has been industry leading for years.

It allows complete voice control of your computer and we mean *complete.* Anything you would do with a mouse you can do with a voice command. Once the system has learned your voice we find that it has unparalleled voice recognition. However, it can get quite expensive. If you are dyslexic, this package may be available to help you study, for free. Talk to the disability centre at your university to find out more.

URL

https://www.nuance.com/en-gb/dragon.html

Other Note Taking Software

Text Compactor

This website takes an input of text and copies and paste all the words you want to condense down into a short summary. You can pick how long you want the summary to be and how much of the original text to keep.

URL

https://www.textcompactor.com/

Evernote Clipper

A chrome extension that allows you to quickly and easily save files, articles, text snippets and quotes to a notes file. Basically, it saves you time on copy and pasting across different note taking platforms as it syncs easily with Evernote's main platform. If you're an Evernote fan then this product really is a no-brainer.

URL

https://chrome.google.com/webstore/detail/evernote-web-clipper/pioclpoplcdbaefihamjohnefbikjilc

Questions to ask yourself before you start taking notes:

1. What is the source of the topic you are taking notes on? (lecture, video, book etc)
2. How much do you need to remember?
3. Will you get a chance to edit and update these at a later date?
4. How fast do you need to take the notes?
5. How are you going to organise your notes?
6. What are the notes going to be used for?
7. Do other people need to understand your notes?

CHAPTER FIVE: PLANNING

Introduction

Planning. Without a doubt, the most underrated and possibly overlooked part of the entire process. Very few people plan, very few people think that they need to plan. However, there are so many benefits to planning an essay.

Firstly, it lays out how you are going to answer the question **before** you start. This makes it easier to check that you are in fact answering the question before you dive in. Secondly, it allows you to easily arrange all your notes into a semi-essay format and, as you won't be searching for notes, or trying to remember what you had thought you were going to say at different points, it will allow you to write much faster. Thirdly, you can pick up from where you left off. Or, in other words, you don't need to write it all in one sitting.

Finally, understanding where you're going and where you've come from, apart from sounding incredibly like a self-help book, is important to your writing. If you want to write better then you need to know how to make your writing flow and the best way to do that is through connecting the different pieces of your essay together succinctly and neatly. This is hard to do on the fly. Not impossible, just difficult. It becomes even more difficult if you don't sit down and write it all in one go, something that you probably can't do if your essay is over 2000 words. Unless, of course, your essay is due in the next day.

Before you dive into the planning, there are a few things that can help you assemble your plan. Once you understand these, you will be able to write significantly better plans and far more persuasive essays.

Before the Plan

The goal of an essay is to persuade the reader - whether that be through the sharing of information and analysis, or the demonstration, exploration or evaluation of a topic. All of these require well written and fluid arguments; they require a building of argument and position. You must convince the reader of your conclusion and the best, and realistically only way to do that, is to present a logical, well-reasoned argument with relevant and specific evidence.

Finding the Argument

The first step to constructing this synergy of logic and reason is to understand what you are arguing for. The question should have given you a good idea of the space you are meant to occupy; your research should have narrowed down the doors you can choose to go through. It is now down to you to think through and decide what line of argument you want to support, what arguments you're going to use to write the critique, how you're going to answer said criticism and on which side, in the final analysis, you will land on.

Normally students do one of two things at this point:

Option 1: They analyse all their research and pick an approach with a lot of content that will be easy to reproduce. They find a line of argument that is well established, with plenty of counter arguments, so they can present an easy, back and forth discussion.

Option 2: They pick a line of argument from their research that interests them. But, as there isn't much information available, they have to work harder to find more analysis, or adapt existing analyses to fit their new arguments, and supplement their own critiques where they can.

Which one do you think is going to get higher marks?

Naturally, option 2 often results in better grades. Now, there is nothing wrong with option 2, but, we believe that there is a third way that lets you add a bit of the fire that sets option 2 apart from option 1.

Option 3: The trick is to do your planning and your research in tandem. Do general, cursory readings first - read abstracts and book introductions to find the arteries of the discussion before digging up the veins. If you have a broad view, you can delve into the topic that interests you. Then, when you're doing your research, you are automatically more motivated by the subject, meaning you'll take more of it in. Further, from this position, it is easier to be specific with your analysis and, if you know what points you are going to argue during your research, the adaptation of other arguments or writing of your critiques can be accomplished far more easily.

Grouping Your Research

Once you've found your argument - either before or after you have finished your research - it is time to start grouping your findings into relevant sections. If there is a debate about a sub-topic in your essay, and you have several commentators on that sub-topic, group those notes together. We've listed some of the general ways to do this below:

- By author: multiple quotes, points or arguments from the same author
- By sub-topic: as we've mentioned; multiple commentators on an issue
- By argument: all research on a specific argument
- By coupled argument: argument points both for and against paired together
- By type:
    - Explanations – of the same thing
    - Arguments – of the same thing
    - Quotes – supporting the same thing

Grouping your notes and research will make it a lot easier when it comes to filling out your plan. You can quickly find similar or opposing ideas, slot them into the flow of your argument, and assign them to paragraphs.

Understanding the Nature of Paragraphs

Before you start making plans for your essay, it is useful to understand how paragraphs are constructed and how to tell a good paragraph from a bad one. Once you know this, it is far easier to allocate information and research to different paragraphs which, in turn, will help when you construct your argument.

A paragraph is essentially a mini-essay. You are introducing a point, making said point, supporting it with evidence before connecting to the next point. Remember, how back in secondary school, you were taught to "**point, quote, explain**" well, this is merely a more in-depth version of that. Do remember however, that you are making **one point** and **one point only**, save the next point for the next paragraph.

Introduction

The introduction to your paragraph is just one sentence (or even part of a sentence). It takes the tail of the last paragraph and adds to it by giving a direct link to what you are going to talk about. The clearer and more concise this sentence is, the easier the reader of your essay will find it to understand the rest of the paragraph. (Just make sure the rest of the paragraph does what you said it would do).

"When looking at the 'figures on the wall' in Plato's allegory of the cave..."

What

The 'what' is simply the point. What are you trying to say, what are you trying to argue? It is, in effect, a mini conclusion. State this conclusion before explaining why and before you set out the evidence to support it.

"You can see that they represent the forms and shapes of items in our world. However, this is not the full intention, new translations originally demonstrate that he intended this to show us specifically 'reflections' rather than the more common interpretation of 'outlines'."

Why

Moving onto the 'why'. Once you've stated your point, you need to explain how it connects to the main topic. Why is it relevant, i.e. if this point is true or false, what are the repercussions for the overall argument?

"This affects the entire interpretation of his initial allegory leading

to a re-evaluation of the relevancy of his theory in the modern world."

How

The 'how' is the meat of the paragraph, this is where you make your case. This is where you need to convince the reader of your argument and share the evidence that supports the 'what' and the 'why'.

If Geoffrey (2018) is correct in his translation then no longer is the allegory of the cave examining the immutable form of things, it's examining the reflection of said forms. It applies a level of distortion that previously was not apparent. This distortion separates the forms from empirical bindings, it retracts the assertions of scholars that "there are no such worlds of forms" (Cole, 1983, pp45) and presents a far more approachable and engaging version of the theory. A reflection is deliberately obscure. In a modern mirror, yes there are clear, perfect reflections, but from the time of Plato there would be nothing of that calibre. There would only have been 'hazy' reflections, a likeness but not perfection.

Connector

The last part of the paragraph needs to be the 'connector', this is the part that leads into the next paragraph. These sentences or parts of sentences create the flow of a good essay - the better your connectors between points, the stronger your argument.

Such an interpretation of the theory creates many opportunities for the application of Plato's work to the modern day.

Outlining in 200 words

If you don't want to write a full plan, or you don't feel that it will help, then writing out a 200-word summary of what you are going to argue can be very helpful. It will help keep you on track and make writing the essay easier; you will be able to track the direction in which you are supposed to be heading. The actual act of writing the summary down is important as it solidifies the essay arguments in your brain.

Structure

The structure of an essay is what makes up the plan. Knowing what goes where and the conventions you need to be aware of are important to consider when writing. A structured plan will help achieve this.

Introduction

The introduction to your essay is your first chance to impress. It is here that you take the hand of the reader and show them in, a broad way, what you are going to talk about. It should give the reader a good idea of where they will be going on their journey and how they are going to get there.

An introduction should be no more than 10% of your total word count. Some people argue that it should never be over 500 words, but we disagree as you cannot introduce a thesis or dissertation that has a total length of 9000 words with only 500. So, we would advise following the 10% rule. It is widely accepted at almost all universities.

Secondly, an introduction should summarise the main arguments in your essay, but not explain the outcome. Use connecting words and phrases like - 'move on', 'continue', 'examine an alternative' or 'investigate the effect'. These will help make the process of describing what you are going to do easier and more succinct.

Depending on your subject and your institution, the jury is out on whether you should state your conclusion directly in the introduction or merely allude to it. Ask your professor for clarification (although both ways tend to work just as well).

Your introduction, then, is basically your plan in condensed form. It takes all your main points, and how they tie together, plus your conclusion and lumps them into the first part of your essay. Thus, you can't really plan your introduction until you've planned your actual essay.

Main Body

The main body of your essay is made up interconnecting paragraphs. Each paragraph represents a point, each point is part of the overall argument. Everything is interlinked, everything should flow. When planning your essay, it is important to remember this as it will help inform where you should place information. For example, a standard format of an essay is:

Introduction

Explanation of the problem/issue - getting the reader on the same page

Argument 1 - Introducing conflict into the scenario

Argument 2 - Offering a contradictory viewpoint to Argument 1

Argument 3 - Either a synthesis of the two previous arguments or a third way that escapes the issues with the first two

Conclusion

This small structure can be broken down into granular arguments and points. But mostly, there is always going to be an argument or a point, then a counter or opposing view, and either a resolution through adaptation or a third argument that brings everything together.

Knowing this makes it easy to construct your plans.

Argument 1: You should write plans because they make your essays better.

Argument 2: You shouldn't write plans because the time would be better spent writing.

Argument 3: You need less time to write with a good plan, and they make your essay better.

If this was a basic argument we could expand this out like so.

Argument 1: You should write plans because they make your essays better.

- How they help
    - Provide structure and organise thoughts
        - Quote from Student 1: how much plans help
    - Make your writing more fluid
        - Quote from Essay writing book: how much plans help

Argument 2: You shouldn't write plans because time would be better spent writing.

- Why you shouldn't
    - The more time you focus on the writing the better
        - Statistics on how increasing the time spent writing improves essays
    - Plans aren't marked
        - Quote from Student 2: how plans take too long and it's your writing that gets marked not your plan.
        - Statistics on the number of plans marked in essays.

Argument 3: You need less time to write with a good plan and it makes your essay better.

- How having a plan reduces time?
  - You know what is coming next and everything is organised
  - Quote from Student 3: how it's quicker to write with a plan
- Students that write plans get better grades
  - Stats on students getting better grades if they plan

This is just slotting in the relevant information to the correct sections from your research. Whilst very few examples will be as simple as this, for example they may have many more than three arguments, the style is the same.

➢ **Note:** Of course, if you have a different type of essay then the outline of the plan will be different. See our templates to get a better understanding of how to plan those.

Remember for each paragraph you need a 'what', a 'why' and a 'how' (plus your introductory sentence and connector, but you won't need to plan those).

- The **what** is your argument's point. What part of the overall argument are you explaining?
- The **why** is why you're doing it. Why is it relevant?
- The **how** is how is it the case. It is the evidence or the reasoning behind it.

Critical Analysis

Typically, to get the best grades, you need to go above and beyond regurgitating other people's arguments or points. Especially in the humanities. You are required to provide your own dissection of the argument at some level - looking for fallacy, points of contention, or providing your own perspective. This is not as simple as writing "I believe x, because y", as a professor is rarely asking for your personal opinion on something.

Rather, they are looking for things like, "due to x, there is y", "after examining x, one is led to conclude y" or "y presents a unique perspective when seen through the lens of x". Avoid using personal pronouns. We'll touch on this later in the writing section but it is worth mentioning here.

When writing your plan, you should be looking for opportunities to inject your own analysis. However, it will be easier to find places to contribute when actually writing. Planning is more of an aerial view and no one expects you to find a massive flaw in a 50-year-old wall, but you might find a small crack that you can make your own.

Conclusion

Planning the conclusion is a must. In fact, if you wrote a 200 word outline of your essay then this could serve as the plan for the conclusion. The key point behind planning the conclusion is to know where you're going. What is the overall goal of the essay? If you know that, then it's just a matter of tracing your way through the paragraphs to reach that conclusion.

Bibliography

Whilst planning the biography sounds stupid, and it is up to an extent, planning what to include in your bibliography sounds less so. Check out the bibliography section for more information on different services you can use to compile a bibliography. But, when it comes to the plan, just keep a note of the resources you have used so far to write your essay.

Example Plan Templates

There are many pre-structured templates or accepted practises for writing essay plans. We have created a tonne and put them into an easy place for you to download them. Visit www.currikula.com/ultimate-essay-guide-resources to access them for free.

CHAPTER SIX: WRITING

Introduction

As an essay writer you have taken notes, and planned and structured the content. Now, it is finally time to start writing. As an essay writer, you are fashioning a series of relevant points into a linear argument that is clear and coherent. Kathy Duffering (1998) from the Harvard Writing Center explains:

> *"Like all human ventures, the conventions of the academic essay are both logical and playful. They may vary in expression from discipline to discipline, but any good essay should show us a mind developing a thesis, supporting that thesis with evidence, deftly anticipating objections or*

counterarguments, and maintaining the momentum of discovery."

The argument, thesis, or question (depending on your subject) of your essay should be original – it is **your** idea that came from conducting outside research. Your argument is backed by supporting points, explained further in the body paragraphs and confirmed in your conclusion.

How can I be original if I am 'given' a topic or question?

We get it, your topic has been written about many times and studied for decades, so coming up with a wholly original argument seems very difficult, even counterintuitive. You can, however, be original in different ways. Expand your reading beyond the original texts, finding inspiration from others who have questioned the argument. Constantly be critical of what others are saying, even scholars. While writing your essay, be mindful of questions from others. Your originality builds the basis for creation of an effective argument.

Critical Analysis

A fundamental difference between higher education and pre-undergraduate education (A-Levels, High School) is the need to be critical of what you read. Summarising a bunch of materials on paper is not enough anymore, and this concept is especially difficult for first year university students who are not used to this type of writing. When reading text that academics have spent years composing, it seems odd to be critical of them. After all, they are supposed to be experts on the subject, right? That's not the point - every argument has aspects that can be debated or at least questioned. Your argument will also have holes (see effective counterargument below), and that is OK. The University of Birmingham supports these examples of critical analysis:

- Engaging with evidence
- Open minded and objective enquiry
- Presenting reasons to dispute a particular finding
- Providing an alternative approach
- Recognising the limitations of evidence: either your evidence or the evidence provided by others
- Thinking around a specific problem

- Applying caution and humility when challenging established positions. Critical writers might tentatively suggest an independent point of view, using such phrases as 'It could be argued that…'; or 'An alternative viewpoint might suggest that…'."

Making Arguments Effective

Your goal is to persuade the reader of your original 'idea'. The 'idea' could be comparing and contrasting two previous arguments in an original way, arguing for or against a particular contention, or bringing new light to an existing argument. Regardless of this 'idea', your argument must be focused, clear, and logical. This section will focus on creating an argument that is clearly structured, connecting topic sentences to your main argument, and maintaining relevance through positive correlation.

Structuring the argument

The 'structure' chapter of this book focused on structuring your essay; this section, however, will focus on structuring your *argument* (and therefore the supporting points).

During your research and note-taking stages, you are likely to have collected material from a variety of sources: books, journals, websites to name a few. Your notes are possibly arranged in the order you started taking them which is, most likely, not the order they need to appear in your argument. They now need to be organised in a more logical order to maximise the effectiveness of your supporting points.

Your first step is to categorise your points generally, removing any that do not fit into a proper category. For a 2000-word essay, the optimal goal is three main categories. If you have a 5000-word essay, you can have four main categories and include more points per category.

A longer essay does not mean you need to have more categories. Some essays require more explanation than others or more in-depth exploration per point.

Once you've identified three to four main categories, you then formalise the specific sub-categories that fit into the larger, general category. For example, if your topic is that Offshore Financial Centres (OFCs) are arguing that they benefit the global economy, the larger general category could be Tax, and your sub-categories could be positive Business Competition, Tax Competition, and Investments. Each subcategory has supporting points that justify it and the overall argument. For example, your supporting points could argue that, by allowing a corporation to reduce its overall tax rate, OFCs help that company compete with other companies with lower statutory tax rates.

Topic – Benefit of OFCs

a) Main Category – Tax

i. Subcategory: Business Competition

Supporting point - Lower tax results in improved business competition between corporations due to less government intervention.

ii. Subcategory: Tax competition forces high tax economies to reduce tax burden in home state

Supporting point – Tax competition increases potential for consumer spending.

Counterargument – Tax competition forces countries to reduce tax to a level that is too low to achieve adequate government revenue.

iii. Subcategory: OFCs allow tax exempt individuals to invest in beneficial funds without acquiring a tax burden.

Supporting point – Some tax burdens are unnecessary where an individual is not resident in a source state and has no obligation to that source state, nor uses its public services.

Note the counterargument in subcategory two. This is an example of a counterargument appearing in the substance of the paragraph itself. See 'An effective counterargument' for more information.

Topic Sentences and clarity

We have often explained the necessity of being clear to your reader and there are few better ways to add clarity than proper use of topic sentences. Not only do topic sentences tell the reader what to expect in each paragraph; they also clearly state the claim and main argument. The paragraph can be full of quotations, supporting explanations, and questions, but the topic sentence(s) have the same goal; to argue. You may have familiarity with a topic sentence at the beginning of each paragraph as an introduction, but that is just one example of their use. Topic sentences can, on occasion, contain multiple sentences. For example, if the first sentence makes a claim, arguing one point, the second sentence may want to explain that claim further, before diving further into the substance of the paragraph. In the example category of taxation, your topic sentence could be:

Lower corporate taxation provides companies with more money to spend on innovation, hire new employees, and improve shareholder value.

While there are several potential formats for topic sentences, the main goal remains to argue the point. This is what brings clarity to the reader, helping them understand your argument. Notice, in the sentence example above, there is a clear claim that lower taxation benefits companies and hurts governments.

Topic Sentences for long essays

What if your essay is not the standard 2000 words, but 5000 words this time? Or, you have a 10,000-word dissertation to write over one year. Each section of your essay consists of multiple paragraphs, even pages. So how do you use topic sentences? Do you have one topic sentence per paragraph or section?

The answer is not to worry; there is no set formula for the perfect topic sentence structure or length. Unless you are in middle school, the hamburger paragraph, which has one topic sentence, three middle sentences, and a conclusion sentence is not the rule. If you have three to four paragraphs covering the same topic, one main topic sentence for the section, with a shorter topic sentence paragraph, is more than enough.

Signposting

If you are writing a longer essay, there is a high chance that you will change direction, even slightly, to cover your topic. The topic sentence shown above is a good example of a change in direction. These direction changes can be in the form of a counterargument, an additional complication to your thesis, or introduce background facts and context (Abrams, 2000). Signposting is one of the most effective mechanisms for shifting direction - a sentence or two that informs the reader of a slight shift in the argument. See the example below for a change in direction that brings additional complications to the thesis:

The ability of multinational companies to reduce their tax liability through offshore financial centres has spurred many of their growths; hiring new employees, spending on innovation, and setting up auxiliary operations in new countries. Meanwhile, governments around the world are trying to tackle the liability avoidance by reducing crucial spending and cutting costs in departments.

These sentences change the direction from arguing the benefits of lower taxes to multinational companies to the burden they have on the government in meeting its revenue and budget goals. Clearly, the next section is going to evaluate the effect of lower taxation on the government.

Signposts can appear as topic sentences, as whole paragraphs, or mid-paragraph. There is no rule that dictates that a change in argument direction must happen at a certain point in the essay; it is all about overall flow and clarity.

An effective counterargument

When writing your essay, it can be useful to introduce a counterargument, which is a logical argument against your essay. The counterargument shows your readers that you have considered possible arguments against your idea, that your idea/thesis is not perfect, and that there are going to be people who question your reasoning. It is the job of the counterargument to anticipate the questions or disagreements a reader may have and explore them in more detail. When using a counterargument, less is more. A counterargument can be used in the introduction to show evidence of why you are arguing your thesis or, within a paragraph, where the supporting points may raise objections but are not be the main focus of your essay. You are, after all, arguing for your idea.

Every effective counterargument has two phases: (1) the point where you turn against your argument, and then (2) turn back to reinforce your argument and refute the counter.

For example, if you are arguing that Brexit was caused by the leave campaign spreading statements that lacked credibility, your counterargument would point to certain evidence that showed some statements could be considered credible. You would then return to your argument by saying many leave voters cast their vote because of the statements lacking credibility (with supporting facts and evidence) and reinforce the argument that Brexit was caused by ill-informed voters.

If you are arguing that the main cause of corporate tax avoidance in the United States (pre-2018) was due to tax rates being too high, your counter argument could point to evidence that tax avoidance was rife after the United States government made its first corporate tax cut from above 50% to 35% in 1993. You would then come back to your initial argument by saying that, even after the cut, it still had one of the highest levels of taxation in the developed world, with complicated and restricting rules and, therefore, tax avoidance was likely to continue.

Argument Clarity

We have referred to the importance of clarity of argument several occasions. If your points are irrelevant or contradictory, they can harm the strength of your argument and your conclusion.

Govier explains how one of the criteria of cogent arguments is relevance; i.e. your supporting points must be **positively** relevant to the argument. The point must count in favour of the argument by providing evidence it is true.

For example:

Smoking produces negative health consequences. The British Heart Foundation found that smokers had a higher risk of developing heart problems.

Exercise is good for one's health. The NHS suggests adults should exercise 150 minutes per week in order to maintain a healthy lifestyle.

On the other hand, **negatively** relevant points can be detrimental to your argument and confuse the reader. They occur when a point provides evidence against the truth of your argument.

Alcohol is bad for one's health. A glass of wine a day keeps the doctor away.

Arguing that a glass of wine a day is healthy contradicts the argument that alcohol is unhealthy and weakens the argument.

Another illustration is **irrelevance,** where your supporting points do not provide reason for or against the argument. An example of this is below:

Smoking is bad for one's health. Cigarette taxation is a major source of revenue for some governments.

The supporting point does not argue that smoking is bad for health nor does it argue against that. The tax revenue from cigarettes does not support the argument about the health effects.

To ensure a clear, concise, and cohesive argument your supporting points need to be positively relevant to the main argument. When editing your essay, look at each supporting point and ask - do the words used clearly support the main argument or could you argue the point more clearly?

Quotations

When making a point, you need to support it with evidence. One way to achieve this is to directly quote a credible source. For example, if your point argued that the US corporate tax system was too uncompetitive pre-2018, you could quote a spokesperson from Microsoft claiming the tax system was unfair to the company:

"Microsoft has a complex business and we must comply with the complicated tax code of the United States, resulting in an exceedingly complex tax structure" (Business Insider, 2013).

A direct quote from a company embroiled in the tax debate of the US is strong supporting evidence to your argument.

When using a quotation, it must be introduced and used properly, not just sit around for the sake of it. Quotations are there to support your points, not make them for you. They should always appear after you have stated your point and agree with what you were saying directly before, i.e. be positively relevant. For example, if you are arguing that the US tax code is unfair using a quotation where the author gives evidence of it being fair, this is confusing and incorrect, even in a counterargument. If used to support your point, it goes against your argument, and shows weakness. If used in a counterargument, you must introduce it properly by stating "there are others who disagree" as this quote shows evidence of the contrary to your argument. See examples below.

Right

The US tax code is inherently complex and restrictive to companies, a spokesperson from Microsoft explains its reason for a complex tax structure; "Microsoft has a complex business and we must comply with the complicated tax code of the United States, resulting in an exceedingly complex tax structure." (Business Insider, 2013)

Microsoft, along with other US multinational companies, claims it is forced to adopt very aggressive tax structures in order to compete with companies that are domiciled in more tax friendly jurisdictions such as the UK, Ireland, and Switzerland.

Wrong

The US tax code is inherently complex and restrictive to companies, a journalist for tax justice (2015) claims, "large multinational companies do not pay their fair share of taxes towards American society". Microsoft, along with other US multinational companies, claims it is forced to adopt very aggressive tax structures in order to compete with companies that are domiciled in more tax-friendly jurisdictions such as the

UK, Ireland, and Switzerland.

- **Note:** The above quote contradicts the point, which is arguing the complexity of the tax system by saying tax avoidance is unfair. This is negative relevance between a point and supporting quotation. If you want to use the journalist's quote to counter your argument, it must be introduced properly first.

Right

The US tax code is inherently complex and restrictive to companies; *however, many do not agree*. A journalist for tax justice (2015) claims, "large multinational companies do not pay their fair share of taxes towards American society". Regardless of what people believe is a company's fair share, Microsoft, along with other US multinational companies, claims it is forced to adopt very aggressive tax structures in order to compete with companies that are domiciled in more tax-friendly jurisdictions such as the UK, Ireland, and Switzerland.

Technical rules surrounding quotations

This just gets more and more fun. You would not believe us, but there are several rules you need to be aware of when using quotations. Better yet, the rules change according to whether you are writing in British or American English. Below are rules we have identified from a variety of sources on how to use quotations properly.

1. Quotation marks are used for direct quotes, to imply alternate meanings, or to emphasise certain words. The most common use of quotations is to directly quote another source. For example, John et al. (2012) said "Paint me a picture with your words.".

2. Direct quotes start with a capital letter only if you are quoting a complete sentence, otherwise no capital letter is required.

3. Every open quotation mark must be closed. "Pictures paint a thousand... needs an ending eventually.

4. If you are writing in British English, then commas, periods, and full stops appear outside of the quotations, however, they appear inside when writing American English.

5. If the punctuation mark applies to the quote, always keep it inside the marks, and outside if not. “Was it true?” John asked. Is it correct in thinking she was truthful when Cassandra mentioned “I was sick during the party”?

6. If you are using a quote within a quote, use single quotation marks. “I am not sure I can fully ‘trust’ him”. Victoria mentioned.

7. You should use a new paragraph for longer quotations of more than 40 words or four lines, and indent the whole section. For example, “Reality is merely an illusion, albeit a very persistent one.”, is a shorter quotation so it appears in this paragraph.

> "A human being is a part of a whole, called by us ‘the universe’, a part limited in time and space. He experiences himself, his thoughts and feelings as something separated from the rest... a kind of optical delusion of his consciousness. This delusion is a kind of prison for us, restricting us to our personal desires and to affection for a few persons nearest to us. Our task must be to free ourselves from this prison by widening our circle of compassion to embrace all living creatures

and the whole of nature in its beauty.",

is a longer quote and requires its own indented paragraph.

8. When introducing a supportive quote as evidence to your argument there are two ways to reference it using parenthetical referencing; introduce the authors directly or indirectly. Indirect introduction involves the author and date/page inside the parenthetical reference; (Smith, 2014). Direct uses the authors name and only the date/page in the parenthesis; Smith (2014) argues.

The following is an example of direct introductions:

Smith (2014) argues the above not to be true, "Positive theorems of relevancy are fundamentally flawed".

Indirectly introducing the quote follows:

"Positive theorems of relevancy are fundamentally flawed," (Smith, 2014).

9. Use when appropriate. Quotations make great supporting evidence, but are not to be used just for the sake of using them. As a rule, you should not have more than half a paragraph of direct quotations. Your paper needs to be original as well. Currikula's analytics identify the proportion of quotations in your paper so you can identify whether you are using too many or not.

Do's and Don'ts of Essay Writing

There are concepts of essay writing where there are no ambiguities. It is a clear yes or no. Below are some examples of things you should and should not do when writing your essay.

Do	Don't
Make your essay easy to read	Use a quote without properly citing the source
Correctly format your essay	Directly address the reader
Use professional vocabulary	Overcomplicate it with fancy words
Cover every aspect of the prompt. If your instructor wants you to evaluate advantages and disadvantages don't just evaluate the former.	Play with formatting to get away with different word count
Reflect on and develop the question	Submit an essay your friend in the year above wrote
Cite every source you use	Copy an essay from online and act as if it's your own
Use Currikula to get feedback	Pay someone else to write your essay

CHAPTER SEVEN: EDITING

Introduction

Now that you have written your essay, it's time to improve it. Editing your essay is arguably just as important as writing it. If you wrote the entire essay over the course of a few nights, you were likely to be so deep in thought that you were not paying full attention and reading it the next day will make you say something like 'did I really write this?'. If your Professor read that essay they will likely think the same. That is why editing is so important. Now that the bulk of the work is done, you can polish, reduce, add, and improve.

The first step in editing your essay is... taking a break. That's right, put your essay away for one day and do not look at it. You need time away from your work to be more objective and critical. This will clear your mind of the deep thought during the period of writing. After a break, you can approach the editing phase with a clear and critical mind.

Read through it once with the following points in mind:

1. Is everything I say related to the main thesis?
2. Are all my points improving my argument?
3. Am I repeating myself often?
4. Does my language sound too complicated?
5. Does every single word belong? Is it making my argument more effective?

If any of the above seem a little off, such as a paragraph that is not relevant to your main argument, or a flurry of sentences that say the same point in multiple different ways, then immediately highlight the problem. If it seems odd during your first read through, the chances are it is. Either highlight the issue in word with changes tracked, or use a highlighter and pen on a printed version – whatever your preference. After your first read through, you'll need to dive deeper into the essay components to make subtler, but important fixes.

Removing Repetition

Repetition comes in many forms; you can start multiple sentences with the same words, repeat multiple sentences, repeat whole paragraphs, and repeat ideas.

In general, you should avoid repetition; it makes your argument and your writing sound less concise. This section will guide you in removing repeated material.

Repeated words

You start every sentence with 'the' or 'if'. You say 'then' three times in one sentence. You start every sentence with the same word (like this paragraph). You accidentally put put two words right after each other.

- **Tip:** When starting a new line in your essay piece, accidentally repeating the word 'the' is a very common mistake that many writers make and very few catch the the error. The most effective way of spotting a double-word repeat is through grammar software, which is discussed later.

Repeated words are technical errors and are easily spotted by grammar software, such as Grammarly, because it is not subject to the flaws of the human eye.

Currikula's analytics software identifies the most used words in your essay, and is also a good place to start when trimming potentially overused words.

Repeated sentences

Repeating the same idea in two sentences is more difficult to spot. In this case below, the sentences are not exact matches, but explain the same idea.

For example:

The team worked very hard to finish their task. Each person in the team worked harder than ever.

Is the second sentence really needed to convey that the team worked very hard? The only exactly repeated term was 'the team worked'. A technical grammar checker is not likely to flag that, and you may want to keep both sentences to reiterate how hard the team worked.

Word Removal

Remove words that are weasel, weak, or unnecessary. Be direct and clear. Every word needs to be vital to conveying the argument.

Modifying Words

Removing Clichés

This point is just the 'tip of the iceberg', or 'let's not push the envelope'. How about 'removing clichés is easier said than done'. Clichés are used *all the time,* and removing them really is *easier said than done.* However, Slick Write, a free service, can identify most clichés in your writing and will help you to *avoid them like the plague*. Currikula will also identify clichés from a list of over 700, including the popular ones such as 'what it boils down to' and 'one in a million'.

This point is just the 'tip of the [illegible] the envelope'. How about 'removing cliches is easier said than done'. Cliches are used all the time, and removing them is rea [illegible] However, Slick Write, a free service discussed earlier, can identify most cliches in your writing and will instruct you to avoid them like the plague. Currikula will also identify cliches from a list of over 700 cliches, including the popular ones such as 'what it boils down to' and 'one in a million'.

Cliché / colloquialism

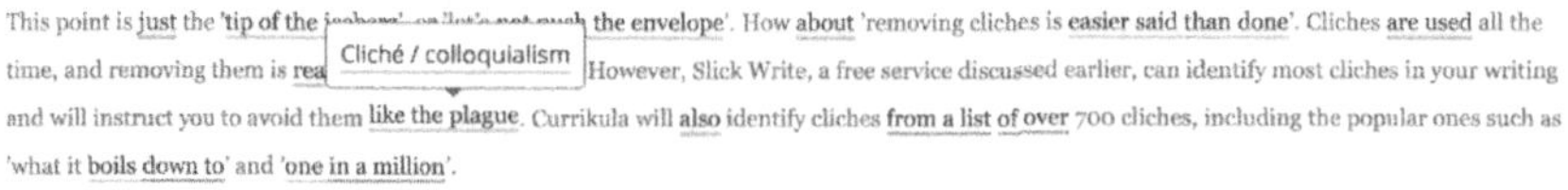

(Slick Write identifying clichés)

Using Professional Academic language

Your essay should be written in language appropriate to your course. For example, if you are a law student then legal language may be appropriate. Whatever your course, the language should always be professional, not colloquial.

Removing jargon, elevated or stilted words and sentences

When you insert a word just to sound impressive, it usually has the opposite effect. For example, "they exited the establishment before engaging in dialogue with the proprietor", can be more effectively explained as "they left the restaurant before speaking with the owner". Elevating the complexity does not make your language sound more academic or professional and will detract from the writing if it sounds out of place.

Flow

Flow is important. Sentences that are the same in length tend to sound monotonous and can put the reader to sleep. In general, you will do this subconsciously. If you discover a lack of variation, then start with short sentences and gradually lengthen them, then shorten again. Then lengthen. Shorten. A good way to check flow is to use Slick Write to see a visual representation of your essay's flow. To shorten long sentences, you can remove words that are unnecessary since longer sentences tend to have more weasel words. Even short changes to sentence length go a long way to improve the flow and interest of your writing.

Spelling

Spelling mistakes are technical errors; there is no debate on the correct or incorrect answer. Every word in your essay needs to be spelled correctly and there are no exceptions. Correcting spelling and grammar mistakes is best done at the very end of your essay, before submission. Our how-to-guide for quickly correcting spelling mistakes is below.

1. Find a system that can identify spelling mistakes with a dictionary. That could be spellcheck on Microsoft Word, Google Docs, or Grammarly.

2. Ensure the dictionary on that spellcheck is set to the correct language. If you are in the UK and writing in English then it should be English (UK). If you are in the US, then set it to American English. British, American, Canadian, and Australian English are all different; behaviour is correct in UK while behavior is correct in US.

3. Run your essay through the spellcheck platform. If this is Microsoft Word then spelling errors are usually highlighted or underlined in red. Grammarly highlights in red as well.

4. Click on every identified spelling error and if it is obviously incorrect, immediately change. If you think spellcheck is

making an error (they sometimes do), then double check using an online dictionary www.dictionary.com and, if you end up correct, click ignore.

5. Ask a friend (preferably one with good spelling skills) to look over your essay and specifically point out spelling errors.

A comparison of the different spelling and grammar checkers can be found later in this chapter. For now, it's useful to know that Microsoft Word and Google Docs spellchecks are less advanced than services such as Grammarly and Writecheck, but they are better than not checking at all. Most spelling and grammar checkers, including Microsoft Word, will check your spelling as you write, but you should always double check your document for highlighted errors.

Grammar

Language grammar, as defined by www.dictionary.com, *is the study of the way the sentences of a language are constructed*. It is about as much fun as it sounds. To make it more fun, grammar is not always technical – there can sometimes be two correct answers. For example, "I bought apples, pears, and plums" is correct as well as "I bought apples, pears and plums". Some writers are eloquent and liberal with grammar while others stick to strict rules. As a student writing an essay we suggest sticking to the rules of grammar. There are hundreds, if not thousands, of rules and it would be silly to list them all here. So, like spelling, we are going to provide a guide on how to best use a grammar checker.

1. Find a system that suits your style and cost preference using our comparisons at the end of the chapter.

2. Go to the settings section of the system. For Grammarly, this is the sidebar of the app. For Microsoft Word this is the spelling and grammar section under preferences. Set your preferences appropriately according to your paper style.

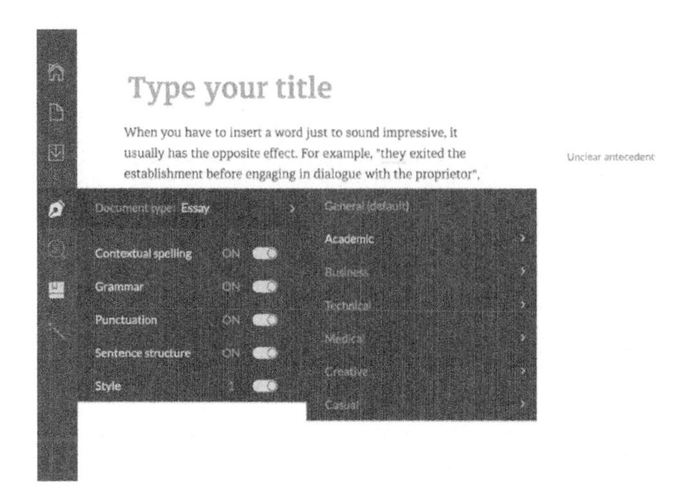

(The Grammarly app editor)

3. Run your essay through the system. All grammar mistakes and suggestions could be highlighted in either yellow, red, or green (Word).

4. Click on any flagged word or phrase. Since errors with grammar are sometimes less obvious than spelling mistakes, you may need to read the phrase a couple of times to understand if the correction makes sense. If you cannot decide, find an answer online. If the suggestion makes practical sense, change it. You can click ignore on every item that is incorrectly identified.

5. Use a friend to proofread your essay with particular attention to grammar. English students are well suited to this.

Readability

Readability is the measurement of how easy your essay is to read and whether someone at a certain reading level could understand it.

You should aim for a readability score appropriate to your audience and your level of study. If you are a university undergraduate then your readability level should reflect that. There are several popular readability formulae, such as the Flesch-Kincaid, which uses sentence length and syllable count to determine the complexity of your writing. The idea is that longer sentences and words with more syllables are more difficult to understand than shorter sentences and fewer syllables. Others, such as the Dale-Chall, use word lists to determine complexity and are commonly used in the science disciplines.

Flesch Formulae

The Flesch Reading Ease formula uses sentence length and syllable count to determine sentence complexity. The formula is as follows:

206.835 - 1.015(total words/total sentences) - 84.6(total syllables/total words)

Below is a table with the conversion of the results

SCORE	SCHOOL LEVEL	NOTES
100.00-90.00	5th grade	Very easy to read. Easily understood by 11-year-old student
90.0–80.0	6th grade	Easy to read. Conversational English for consumers
80.0–70.0	7th grade	Easy to read for most people
70.0–60.0	8th & 9th grade	Plain English. Easily understood by 13- to 15-year-old students
60.0–50.0	10th to 12th grade	A reasonably complex piece of writing
50.0–30.0	College	Difficult to read
30.0–0.0	College graduate	Very difficult to read. Best understood by university graduates

The Flesch-Kincaid Grade level formula uses the same information as reading ease but calculates a grade level rather than a score.

0.39(total words/total sentences) +11.8(total syllables/total words) -15.59

This equation outputs the grade level required to have a good understanding of what has been written.

Dale-Chall

The Dale-Chall formula, uses a word list of 3000 words understood by 80% of fourth grade students. It calculates a raw score using the percentage of words not found on the list from samples of 100 words throughout the text as well as average sentence length.

0.1579*(PDW) + 0.0496*(ASL) + 3.6365

And below the easy score conversion below:

DALE-CHALL RAW SCORE	FINAL SCORE
4.9 AND BELOW	Grade 4 and below
5.0–5.9	Grades 5–6
6.0–6.9	Grades 7–8
7.0–7.9	Grades 9–10
8.0–8.9	Grades 11–12
9.0–9.9	Grades 13–15 (college)
10 AND ABOVE	Grades 16 and above.

Calculating Readability Scores

The best way to calculate your readability score is by uploading your essay to an online site. If you would like to compare your Currikula reading score with that of others then you can upload your paper on www.currikula.com after creating an account. In addition to providing you with analytics, Currikula will also provide feedback specifically tailored to your essay.

Applying your Readability Score

Once you have received your readability score, whether from the Flesch-Kincaid, Currikula, or another source, you need to interpret it to make improvements. For example, if you score below 40 on the Flesch Reading Ease formula and you are writing a first-year undergraduate paper, it is likely your essay writing is too complex. If you scored below a 7 on the Dale-Chall, it would be considered too simple for undergraduate level.

So, how do you improve your essay to make it readable for the correct audience if there is a mismatch? Well, a common factor across most formulae is average sentence length or ASL. The longer your sentences, the more complex your writing. The easiest way to simplify your writing is to remove extra or unnecessary words in your writing. We've also discussed this approach to improve your writing in general.

The readability formulae are around 90-95% accurate with reading tests, so they provide a good indicator of writing complexity, however, they are not perfect. You should always try to maintain variation in sentence length and word choice, present clear and concise arguments, and maintain relevancy, as discussed above.

Professional Editing Software

There are over a dozen powerful editing sites out there that use machine learning, algorithms, and rules to identify spelling and grammatical errors in your essay. The best part is – most are free to some extent. They pay particular attention to spelling and grammar and are more advanced than spellcheck. This section analyses and evaluates five different editing sites so that you can choose the one that's right for you.

1. Grammarly

A free, easy to use and intelligent spelling and grammar checker. This is rated as the best overall and is a high-level spelling and grammar improver. Grammarly uses artificial intelligence and patented technology to make much better improvements to your writing than Microsoft Word. You can also upgrade to a premium version (albeit at a high cost) to get plagiarism checks and advanced improvements. Grammarly consistently flaunts its ability to catch writing errors that other writing checkers cannot and has received two patents for its technology (as of this date). Visit its website www.grammarly.com to start editing your essay.

Grammarly premium checks for problems in five main categories:

i. Contextual Spelling

ii. Grammar

iii. Punctuation

iv. Sentence Structure

v. Style

In addition, there is an option to add vocabulary enhancement, which suggests alternative synonyms for overused words and adds diversity to your writing.

Grammarly is not perfect, however. For example, the sentence 'I like watching movies TV shows plays and music' was not identified as requiring commas when we checked.

Grammarly premium will also check for plagiarism, but it won't automatically cite and add found sources to your bibliography. Refer to our referencing chapter for more information on referencing and your bibliography.

Grammarly is offered as a monthly subscription, at US$29.95 per month. Discounts are available if you purchase a quarterly or annual plan and pay up front. Quarterly becomes US$19.98

per month if you pay US$59.95 up front and annual is $11.66 per month if you pay US$139.95 up front.

2. Slick Write

Slick Write is a free application that checks your writing for grammatical errors, potential stylistic issues, and highlights the flow and structure of your essay.

At first it seems complicated, so taking the quick tutorial is a good idea for first time users.

After you have uploaded your paper, the first screen is the critique slide, which highlights suggestions under each word. You can click each word for more information on the suggestion.

One feature of Slick Write is that it also has a basic analytics overview of your writing, which comprises:

a) passive voice index

b) prepositional phrase index

c) automated reading index

d) vocabulary variety

e) adverbs

f) function words

g) sentence breakdown

The sentence 'I like watching movies TV shows plays and music' was not identified as requiring commas.

Explanations are found for every suggestion and more detail is provided in the help section.

Slick Write gives abundant amounts of feedback, both technical and fundamental. It operates on the principle 'more is better', and advises in some of its suggestions that you can take the advice sparingly. For example, it highlights every possible adverb, advising that around 5% is an appropriate proportion of adverbs in a document.

Slick Write also checks the flow of the essay, showing structural flow, sentence length flow, and word length flow. A general tip is that variety is preferred, and variety is shown by wavy lines.

You can access Slick Write at www.slickwrite.com

3. Write Check

WriteCheck is built by iParadigms, the sister site of every students least favourite program, Turnitin. The most logical reason you may want to choose WriteCheck is not its grammar and spellchecking capabilities but it's originality checking system, which uses the same algorithms and database as Turnitin. Basically, it is a failsafe method for passing the Turnitin plagiarism check which your university may use. More on this will be covered in the plagiarism section of this chapter.

The WriteCheck service comprises of three sections: plagiarism checker, grammar checker, and tutoring (optional).

The grammar checker highlights mechanical issues such as fused or compound words, style concerns such as passive voice, and usage areas such as faulty comparisons and confused words. They claim to use the Educational Testing Service (ETS) e-rater technology, a Natural Language Processing tool to evaluate the essay. This fact could make WriteCheck more appropriate for certain essays, however, this is highly biased towards writing in the US.

WriteCheck has no free version or monthly subscription and you will pay per paper uploaded, at $7.95 per paper. You can upload the same paper three times, as long as it is 80% similar to the last version. If you want a professional tutor to edit your work, it costs $29.95 per paper.

Visit the site at www.writecheck.com

4. Bibme

Bibme is a Chegg service, originally part of ImagineEasy solutions. It is a sister site to CiteThisForMe and Easybib, all with similar citation features. However, Bibme offers a pro version which checks your paper for $9.99 USD per month or a light version offering more limited checks.

For free, you can get 20 suggestions per paper on improving sentence structure, punctuation, writing style, and grammar, as well as adding citations to your bibliography, much like their other sites.

The premium version offers everything the free version has but with unlimited writing suggestions and unlimited plagiarism checks.

Like other solutions, the writing suggestions raise issues with passive voice, punctuation, and word use.

Bibme is $9.99 per month and there is no fixed contract like Grammarly. You have unlimited usage for the month and can cancel anytime.

You can check it out here: https://www.bibme.org/grammar-and-plagiarism/

5. Hemingway

Hemingway App is an easy-to-use, powerful writing editor. It is available as both a free and premium version, although the editing technology is the same for both versions.

Hemingway has aspects that make it unique to all other editors.

i. You can write directly in the editor with **bold,** *italic,* and other formatting. Suggestions will appear as you write.

ii. You can hide the suggested edits while you write.

iii. The premium version allows you to work without an internet connection (all others are only web-based).

iv. Hemingway allows for export to Microsoft Word and other formats after editing, while most other only do .txt.

As far as the editing function goes, the app is very simple. It highlights complex sentences, adverbs, and passive voice. Spelling and grammar are not part of the app. The sentence 'I like watching movies TV shows plays and music' was not identified as requiring commas.

It is available here: http://www.hemingwayapp.com/

Comparison

CATEGORY	Spelling	Grammar	Advanced Grammar (structure, style)	Vocabulary help	Citation	Edit while writing	Overall Analytics	Plagiarism	Exporting power	Cost for premium
HEMINGWAY	No	Yes	Yes	No	No	Yes	No	No	High	**$19.99 once**
BIBME	Yes	Yes	Yes	No	Yes	No	No	Premium	Low (Word only)	**$9.99/m**
WRITECHECK	Yes	Yes	Yes	No	No	No	No	Yes	N/A	**$7.99/paper**
SLICK WRITE	No	Yes	Yes	Yes	No	No	Yes	No	Low (.txt only)	**Free only**
GRAMMARLY	YES	YES	YES	YES	NO	YES	NO	PREMIUM	Low (.txt only)	**$29.99/M**

Plagiarism

Plagiarism. The word can generate the same reaction as hearing the name 'Voldemort'. Plagiarism is an act or instance of using or closely imitating the language and thoughts of another author without authorisation and the representation of that author's work as your own, and not crediting the original author. You can plagiarise in several ways:

1. Having someone else write your essay and passing the work off as your own (even with their permission). A popular example is the use of Essay Mills.

2. Submitting a previously written essay and passing it off as your own.

3. Using material from books, articles, or other material without proper quotes or references.

4. Forgetting to reference a quote.

5. Your writing has strong similarities to another without your knowledge and is unreferenced.

Unfortunately, many plagiarism cases are accidental but, nonetheless, treated with severe punishments. They could range from grade penalties to suspension or total expulsion depending on the case. Your university or college is likely to use a similarity checker to detect suspicious material, the most popular being Turnitin. These systems are getting more robust every year, with Turnitin saving all submitted essays for future similarity checking. Currently your essay will be checked against over 50 billion webpages, 110 million journal articles, and over 600 million previously submitted essays globally.

Methods (1) and (2) are clearly academic dishonesty. We are strongly against people falsly claiming ideas or work as their own, and thus we will not refer to them again.

Methods (3), (4), and (5) are all likely to be solved if a reference is correctly made. Our best guidance is to reference more than less. That is why Currikula has a Smart Source feature which uses similarity checking technology to find references that you may have forgotten, lost or not known about, for your essay.

We have dedicated a whole chapter to referencing, including the different styles and formats, so this section is designed specifically for referencing to avoid accidental plagiarism.

How to check your text for proper referencing

There are large discrepancies between similarity checkers and human readers, meaning a similarity checker may identify suspicious text while your instructor will not and vice versa. To be completely safe, your essay should pass both the robotic checker and the human test. Our guide to ensuring the least chance of suspicious text is as follows:

1. Run through your text and identify all direct quotes. These should all have in-text references next to them. If they do not, then it is a red flag. Find where the quote came from and insert the reference accordingly. For more information on formatting please see referencing chapter.

2. Read your essay a second time, this time looking for paragraphs that seem light on referencing. Any paragraph with over ten sentences and no references could have supporting material from other authors and require a reference. There are exceptions, but we suggest it is better to be safe than sorry.

3. Upload your essay to an online plagiarism checker. Depending on the importance of your essay (if it is a 10,000 word dissertation or 1,000 word personal reflection), you may want to spend money using a quality service such as WriteCheck. Any identified text should be looked at more

thoroughly and referenced if required. Currikula's Smart Source feature will let you add found references directly to your bibliography (but you will still have to reference in-text manually).

If you satisfy all three criteria above, chances are your paper is correctly referenced and you can be comfortable submitting to Turnitin or your university's equivalent.

CHAPTER EIGHT: REFERENCING

Introduction

Referencing, while it may be a student's worst nightmare, is an important and necessary part of academia. It can cause you lots of trouble if not done correctly, but is not as difficult as it sounds. In academia, you are almost certainly going to reference other authors' work and, therefore, will need to correctly give credit to such sources. This is likely to be in the form of in-text citations and a full list of references at the end of the essay, sometimes called a bibliography. There are four main styles of referencing, Harvard, APA, MLA, and Chicago. This chapter will explain the similarities and differences between them and provide a step by step guide how to use them to reference your work.

An important concept of referencing is knowing its purpose: to give credit where it is due and make it easy for the ready to identify and find the source if desired. With this in mind, we know that regardless of style and source type there are several key pieces of information that make up a reference. The first is **the creator(s**) - readers want to know who produced the material you are referencing. The creator takes different forms, such as the author, filmmaker, speaker, or interviewer. Regardless of what, whom, or style you are referencing, you can be almost certain the creator is part of the required reference. The next is the **date.** This is important; the reader/instructor wants to know if you are sourcing information from recently or 100 years ago (most material should be less than ten years old unless you are a history student or it is course material). The final element is the **title.** This is likely to be the most easily identifiable piece of information about common sources. There are several other entries that are required depending on the source type and referencing style, such as URL for websites, DOI for journals, and publisher for books, but you will find the **creator, date, and title** in almost every reference regardless of style or source.

- **Top Tip –** If you need clarification on a particular reference ask your professor. An answer from the person marking your essay will guarantee you get it right and, if you get it in writing (an email), then you have proof. When in doubt, include more information in your reference instead of less. We will continuously give this advice throughout the chapter.

Harvard Referencing

Harvard style referencing is very common among a wide range of university courses and uses parenthetical referencing. Key components of the Harvard System are:

i. In-text citations are included in the paragraphs alongside the sentence that is supported by the reference. They use parentheses to house the author(s)' last name(s) and date separated by a comma. An example is (John, 2017).

ii. The Harvard System uses a reference list over a bibliography. This means all sources in your reference list must have an in-text citation. Please check with your instructor as some course requirements slightly differ from conventional methods. More about reference list vs bibliography can be found in the section *Bibliography vs Reference list.*

iii. References are listed in alphabetical order using the authors' **Last Name.**

Harvard In-Text Citations

In-text citations are used when directly referring to the source material. They are located in the body of the work and contain part of the full citation, the author and date.

Depending on the source type and number of authors, some Harvard reference in-text citations may look something like this:

Hermione, Harry, and Ron fought off the troll in the dungeon (Rowling, 1998).

If there are multiple authors, you just list them in the order they are displayed in the text.

Three authors

(Bardes, Shelley, and Schmidt, 2011)

Four or more authors after the first citation

(Potter et al., 2013)

No authors

If there are no authors then you may include the title of the book in place of the author

(Title of book, date)

(To Kill a Mockingbird, 1960)

*To Kill a Mockingbird does have an author (Harper Lee) this is only for display purposes

The et al. rule

There is a confusing debate about how to cite multiple authors in-text, and when you should use 'et al.' (and others). Some guides say three or more authors is acceptable, while others say four or more. Some say you should list all of the authors the first time (even if there are six!) and then use et al. for all subsequent citations. You can always check with your instructor to find the right answer for your course, but our best advice is to be most cautious. You are less likely to be penalised for giving too much information in your references than giving less.

Our guide to being cautious is the following: If there are three authors or less you always list all three, for the first and all subsequent. If there are four or more, the first citation lists all authors, even if there are ten (unlikely ever to be more than six). Afterwards, all subsequent citations can use 'et al.'.

Harvard Reference List – Complete Citations

While there are over 20 different types of sources you can reference through Harvard, the most common forms in the UK for Harvard are books, journal articles, and websites. This section will focus on reference formatting for the three common sources. If you are referencing a less common source, such as a podcast or court case, please search for a specific formatting guide online.

Books – basic format

Reference lists for Harvard are included at the end of your work and include full source details presented in the following basic format:

> Author Last name, First Initial. (Year published). *Title*. City: Publisher, Page(s).

These are fully completed references that link back to your in-text citations. The detail about the source provides the reader with more information about your research.

This chapter includes citation guides for common formats, you can find more information online for specific cases, such as chapters and edited books with multiple editors.

Books with one author

> Author, Initials. (Year). *Title of book.* Edition. (only include this if not the first edition) Place of publication (this must be a town or city, not a country): Publisher, page.

Example

> Kolhatkar, S. (2017). *Black Edge: Inside Information, Dirty Money, and the Quest to Bring Down the Most Wanted Man on Wall Street*. 1st ed. New York: Random House, pp.5-10.

Books with multiple authors

For books with multiple authors, **all*** the names should all be included in the order they appear in the document. Use **'and'** to link the last two multiple authors.

**This is different to in-text citations where 'et al' can be used. Do not get confused and think you can use 'et al' for book sources in your reference list!*

Three authors and third edition

Barker, R., Kirk, J. and Munday, R.J. (1988). *Narrative analysis.* 3rd ed. Bloomington: Indiana University Press, pp.45-112.

Five authors and first edition

Vermaat, M., Sebok, S., Freund, S., Campbell, J. and Frydenberg, M. (2014). *Discovering computers*. Boston: Cengage Learning, pp.32, 44, 56.

Articles from journals and magazines

Scholarly articles are found in academic journals and, depending on your course and institution, you may be accessing them from your online library or a print source. They generally follow the same format as books, with in-text citations formatted exactly the same way. In your full citation, pay attention to the volume and issue number, which is inserted after the title. This is the 'edition' of the journal.

Articles from printed sources – basic journal reference

The required elements for a reference are: Author, Initials., Year. Title of article. *Full Title of Journal,* Volume number (Issue/Part number), Page number(s).

For example:

> Hamel, G. and Prahalad, C. (1985). Do you really have a global strategy?. *The International Executive*, 27(3), pp.13-14.

Electronic journal articles

Most of the time you can reference an e-journal article as print if it is also available in a print version of the journal. This is usually the case where you access an article in pdf format and it uses sequential journal page numbers.

> Hamel, G. and Prahalad, C. (1985). Do you really have a global strategy?. *The International Executive*, 27(3), pp.13-14.

To be safe, you can also add the electronic details, which is the date (different from date published) and the online library you accessed it from.

Articles from a Library database

For articles accessed through a password protected database from the University Library:

> Author, Initials. (Year). Title of article. *Full Title of Journal,* [type of medium] Volume number (Issue/Part number), Page numbers if available. Available through: University of Exeter Library website <http://lib.exeter.ac.uk> [Accessed date].

For example:

> Hamel, G. and Prahalad, C. (1985). Do you really have a global strategy?. *The International Executive*, [e-journal] 27(3), pp.13-14. Available through: University of Exeter Library website <http://lib.exeter.ac.uk> [Accessed 15 July 2017].

Articles publicly available on the internet

If you have found the article from the web, then you can include the URL instead of the university library site, but you still need to include the access date.

> Authors, Initials. (Year). Title of article. *Full Title of Journal or Magazine,* [online] Available at: web address (quote the exact URL for the article) [Accessed date].

For example:

> Kipper, D. (2008). Japan's new dawn. *Popular Science and Technology,* [online] Available at:<http://www.popsci.com/popsci37b144110vgn/html> [Accessed 22 June 2009].

Articles with DOIs

You can choose to use the DOI (Digital Object Identifier) instead of the format/location/access date. The DOI is a permanent identifier and replaces a permanent web address for online articles. It is often found at the start/end of an article or on the database landing page for the article. Not all articles are assigned a DOI. If an article does not have a DOI, use one of the other e-journal article formats. If you have a DOI, you do not need to include the date accessed as the DOI provides the information for the exact source you used.

> Author, Initials. (Year). Title of article. *Full Title of Journal,* [e - journal] Volume number (Issue/Part number), Page numbers if available. DOI.

For example:

> Hamel, G. and Prahalad, C. (1985). Do you really have a global strategy?. *The International Executive,* [e-journal] 27(3), pp.13-14. DOI: 10.1002/tie.5060270306

Websites

Websites are similar to books, where the author comes first, then the date and title. With websites, you are likely going to include the URL rather than the publisher as well as the date you accessed the website. You can also include the name of the website.

> Author Surname, Author Initial. (Year). *Title*. [online] Website Title. Available at: <http://Website URL> [Accessed Date Accessed].

In this example, Bloomberg.com is the name of the website which published the article.

> Finch, G. (2018). *Banking Giants Step Up Pre-Brexit Frankfurt Hires*. [online] Bloomberg.com. Available at: <https://www.bloomberg.com/news/articles/2018-01-12/goldman-sachs-morgan-stanley-step-up-pre-brexit-frankfurt-hires> [Accessed 12 Jan. 2018].

APA Style

The APA style of referencing is another form of parenthetical referencing, similar to the Harvard style. Developed by the American Psychology Association, it is found most commonly in social and behavioural sciences; however, you should always check with your professor which style you need to use.

APA has some similarities to Harvard referencing:

i. In-text citations are included in the paragraphs alongside the sentence that is supported by the reference, using parenthesis to house the author(s) last name(s) and date separated by a comma. An example is (John, 2017).

ii. The APA System uses a reference list over a bibliography. This means all sources in your reference list must have an in-text citation. Please check with your professor as some course requirements slightly differ from conventional methods. More about reference list vs bibliography is found in the section *Bibliography vs Reference list*.

iii. References are listed in alphabetical order from the authors

Last Name

APA has a few subtle differences to Harvard which are sometimes difficult to realise, so be careful when switching between the two for different subjects.

Differences between APA and Harvard

1. APA uses 'References' instead of 'Reference list' to title the list of references.

2. In the APA system the page numbers are cited before the publisher and place of publication rather than at the end and appear in parenthesis.

APA In-text Citations

When referencing in-text citations, APA follows a similar format to Harvard. Citations are inserted directly at the end of the sentence that they are supporting.

For example:

> It is argued that the company did not do enough to cover its social responsibility policies (Smith, 2017).

Multiple Authors

The APA Style Organisation (yes there is such a thing) suggests the **'et al.'** rule be applied like the following table.

Number of authors	First text citation (either parenthetical or narrative)	Subsequent text citations (all)
One or two	Palmer & Roy, 2008	Palmer & Roy, 2008
Three, four, or five	Sharp, Aarons, Wittenberg, & Gittens, 2007	Sharp et al., 2007
Six or more	Mendelsohn et al., 2010	Mendelsohn et al., 2010

Although this is less cautious than our 'cautious rule' (where we say you can use et al. on the first text citation of six or more authors) you are likely to be safe using the above. Like always, check with your professor if you have any doubts. **As always, 'et al.' should not appear in your reference list (all authors must appear listed).**

APA Reference List Formatting

Books – basic format

Author, A. (Year of Publication). *Title of work*. Publisher City, (page numbers if applicable) State: Publisher.

Books with one author

Kolhatkar, S. (2017). *Black Edge: Inside Information, Dirty Money, and the Quest to Bring Down the Most Wanted Man on Wall Street* (pp. 5-10). New York: Random House.

Books with two authors

Kolhatkar, S., & Smith, J. (2017). *Black Edge: Inside Information, Dirty Money, and the Quest to Bring Down the Most Wanted Man on Wall Street* (pp. 5-10). New York: Random House.

*Note some references in this guide do not refer to a particular work and have additional information for display purposes only.

Books with three authors

Ginzburg, C., Tedeschi, J., & Tedeschi, A. (2003). *The cheese and the worms*. Baltimore, Md.: Johns Hopkins University Press.

Websites – basic format

Author, A. (date). Title of document [Format description]. Retrieved (full date), from https://website.example/url

Finch, G., & Arons, S. (2018). *Banking Giants Step Up Pre-Brexit Frankfurt Hires*. Bloomberg.com. Retrieved 12 January 2018, from https://www.bloomberg.com/news/articles/2018-01-12/goldman-sachs-morgan-stanley-step-up-pre-brexit-frankfurt-hires

Journal Article - offline

Last name, Initial(s)., & Last name, Initial(s). (Year). Article title. *Journal Title*, *Volume Number* (issue or part number if needed), page numbers.

For example:

Hamel, G., & Prahalad, C. (1985). Do you really have a

global strategy?. *The International Executive*, *27*(3), 13-14.

Journal Article - online

Last name, Initial(s)., & Last name, Initial(s). (Year). Article title. *Journal Title, Volume Number*(Issue or part number if needed*)*, page numbers. DOI or Retrieved from URL and date

For example:

Hamel, G., & Prahalad, C. (1985). Do you really have a global strategy?. *The International Executive*, *27*(3), 13-14. http://dx.doi.org/10.1002/tie.5060270306

*As with Harvard, if you have a DOI then no date accessed is required. A DOI can technically identify the material without any other information required.

MLA Style

The good old Modern Language Association, founded in 1883, has a referencing style used commonly by English and Literature students. This style is meant to be simpler than Harvard and APA and has a few distinct differences.

1. In-text citations do not include the date but rather the page number. (Smith, 2010) becomes (Smith 12). There is no comma between the author or page number like in APA and Harvard.

2. If you are citing a non-print source without a page number, you only include the author or the first piece of information that appears in your full reference.

3. MLA makes use of the term 'container'. While possible in other styles, container is much more common in MLA and refers to any print or digital work that is part of a larger body of work. A single poem contained in a larger body of poems would have the body of poems as the container. For example, Poem #4 in 'Shakespeare's 10 best poems' would have 'Shakespeare's 10 best poems' as the container. If you are referencing a YouTube video then YouTube would be the container. If you are referencing a newspaper article, the newspaper would be the container. A website name would be the container for the website.

Reference list – full citations

Book

As MLA is used primarily in English and Literature courses, books and literary sources are the most commonly cited and, as it is designed to be simpler than other styles, there is no need to include the city or state of the publisher.

> Last Name, First Name. *Title of Book*. Publisher, Publication Date.

For example:

> Kolhatkar, Sheelah. *Black Edge: Inside Information, Dirty Money, And The Quest To Bring Down The Most Wanted Man On Wall Street*. Random House, 2017.

Another major difference is when there are multiple authors; it is acceptable to use 'et al.' in the reference list if there are three or more authors, supposedly making it a friendlier style.

For example:

Wysocki, Anne Frances, et al. *Writing New Media: Theory and Applications for Expanding the Teaching of Composition*. Utah State UP, 2004.

Two authors

However, if there are two authors, both must be listed.

Kolhatkar, Sheelhah, and John Smith. *Black Edge: Inside Information, Dirty Money, And The Quest To Bring Down The Most Wanted Man On Wall Street*. New York: Random House, 2017. Print.

If you are an English or Literature student there is a high chance you will be citing a poem, short story, or anthology.

A Work in an Anthology, Reference, or Collection

Works may include an essay in an edited collection or anthology or a chapter of a book. For example, if you are in a poetry class, you could have an assignment on European Poetry and have to reference multiple European Poems from one collection. The basic form for this sort of citation is as follows:

Last name, First name. "Title of Essay." *Title of Collection*, edited by Editor's Name(s), Publisher, Year, Page range of entry. Some examples:

> Harris, Muriel. "Talk to Me: Engaging Reluctant Writers." *A Tutor's Guide: Helping Writers One to One*, edited by Ben Rafoth, Heinemann, 2000, pp. 24-34.

> Swanson, Gunnar. "Graphic Design Education as a Liberal Art: Design and Knowledge in the University and The 'Real World.'" *The Education of a Graphic Designer*, edited by Steven Heller, Allworth Press, 1998, pp. 13-24.

Poem or Short Story Examples

Burns, Robert. "Red, Red Rose." *100 Best-Loved Poems,* edited by Philip Smith, Dover, 1995, p. 26.

Kincaid, Jamaica. "Girl." *The Vintage Book of Contemporary American Short Stories*, edited by Tobias Wolff, Vintage, 1994, pp. 306-07.

If the specific literary work is part of the author's own collection (all of the works have the same author), then there will be no editor to reference:

For example:

Whitman, Walt. "I Sing the Body Electric." *Selected Poems*. Dover, 1991, pp. 12-19.

Carter, Angela. "The Tiger's Bride." *Burning Your Boats: The Collected Stories*. Penguin, 1995, pp. 154-69.

Journals and periodicals

Journals and periodicals tend to have more information than books, with multiple contributors and containers. When citing journals and periodicals in MLA, use the following format:

> Author. Title. Title of container (self-contained if book), Other contributors (translators or editors), Version (edition), Number (vol. and/or issue no.), Publisher, Publisher Date, Location (pp. pages used).

Website

Websites fall under the 'electronic sources' category of MLA.

Online guides suggest the following general format when citing an electronic source:

> Author. Title. Title of container (website, online journal, etc.), Other contributors (translators or editors if available), Version (edition if applicable), Number (vol. and/or no.), Publisher, Publication Date, Location (pages, paragraphs and/or URL, DOI or permalink).

More specifically, the format for a website is as follows:

> Editor, author, or compiler name (if available). Name of Site. Version number (if available), Name of institution/ organisation affiliated with the site (sponsor or publisher), date of resource creation (if available), URL, DOI or permalink. Date of access (if applicable).

You will notice there is a lot of 'if available'. It is always good to include as much information as possible, but don't worry if you can't find specific details. Online sources don't follow the same structure as books and some information is just not there.

You will also notice that each piece of information can potentially go by several different titles, for example 'Location' could be URL, pages, DOIs, or permalink. You only need to include one.

A website reference, when finished, looks like this:

> Felluga, Dino. Guide to Literary and Critical Theory. Purdue U, 28 Nov. 2003, www.cla.purdue.edu/english/theory/. Accessed 10 May 2006.

Not too bad, right?

Periodicals and Journals

In MLA, periodicals include magazines, newspapers, and scholarly journals. Cited entries for periodical sources include three main elements — the author of the article, the title of the article, and information about the magazine, newspaper, or journal. Containers are more common here as books are usually self-contained.

The following format is suggested for periodicals and journals.

> Author. Title. *Title of container.* Other contributors (translators or editors if applicable), Version (edition), Number (vol. and issue no.), Publisher, Publisher Date, Location (pp.).

For example:

Bagchi, Alaknanda. "Conflicting Nationalisms: The Voice of the Subaltern in Mahasweta Devi's Bashai Tudu." *Tulsa Studies in Women's Literature*, vol. 15, no. 1, 1996, pp. 41-50.

Hamel, Gary, and C. K. Prahalad. "Do You Really Have A Global Strategy?." *The International Executive*, vol 27, no. 3, 1985, pp. 13-14.

Universal concepts between all three styles

While Harvard, APA, and MLA all have style differences (after all they were produced by different organisations for different purposes), there are some significant universal concepts that apply to all referencing which will help you determine if your reference is appropriate or not.

1. You need to include whoever created the source. Whether it's the author, editor, or filmmaker, someone created the material you are referencing and you need to credit that person.

2. Every piece of work should have a title of some sort. Whether it's a website, book, or journal, titles make it easy to identify common and credible sources.

3. Dates are important, but differ between courses and styles. It is assumed you will be referencing century old Shakespeare texts in English, and maybe millennial old text in Classic History, but in courses such as finance, marketing, and management, recent texts are usually preferred. Even if you are referencing a historic event, the article, book, or website is likely to be less than twenty years old. There are, of course, exceptions. Regardless of whether a specific date is appropriate for your course, listing the date in the reference

list is important.

The three pieces of information above are of significance when compiling your reference list. Including the author is much more important to your instructor than whether the title is italicised or not.

Bibliography vs Reference List

You will constantly hear these two terms used interchangeably, but there is a difference between a reference list and a bibliography. Make sure you know which one is required in your course. A reference list is a list of sources that have been officially cited in your text, while a bibliography includes your full list of in-text references **plus** all references that you read and took inspiration from. This includes any books, articles, websites, films, and any other sources you read, watched, or listened to while researching and writing your essay. These sources are referenced the same way as in a reference list and appear in your bibliography depending on the method of referencing.

Using an auto-citation machine

Auto-citation machines can be beneficial. Likely you or a friend has used them at least once before. They not only format your reference according to source type and style but, in some cases, they can create the citation with just one piece. For example, you type in 'Harry Potter', and they find J.K. Rowling as the author, the Philosopher's Stone as the title, and 1999 as the date. You click auto-cite and voila – you have your reference. They can do this with websites and books as well. This makes referencing much easier, but there are some points you should be aware of.

1. When you cite a source, especially a website, not all information is likely to be found. The above is especially true for the author or title. If your reference looks short and doesn't have a name at the beginning, it is likely missing some information.

2. There are likely to be multiple versions or types of the same reference for books and journals. The system they use takes information from a massive database which is updated continuously from libraries around the world, so there is likely to be multiple editions of a book or journal. Make sure you choose the right one. For example, auto-citing 'Harry Potter

and the Philosopher's Stone' on a popular site returns ten results on the free version, all of which have slightly different information. Make sure you choose the right reference and fill in any missing information.

3. Make sure you select the correct style. Many machines have hundreds of different styles and editions (MLA has eight versions and APA has 6).

Credible vs Non-credible sources

Most students have heard their professors say 'never cite Wikipedia'. While there is nothing wrong with Wikipedia, it is considered a non-credible source by most institutions due to the fact others (non-academics) can edit the information. There are many other sources that professors may also consider not credible and the list is continually updated. In light of this, we have compiled a list of sources into a blacklist. Blacklist sources are considered unreliable by academic professors and should not appear in your reference list or bibliography.

Our Reference Blacklist

www.wikipedia.com

www.investopedia.com

www.facebook.com

www.twitter.com

www.instagram.com

www.blogger.com

www.medium.com

www.tumblr.com

www.pinterest.com

*Naturally there are exceptions to this rule if you are deliberately referring to something sourced from one of these sites. But generally they should not be used.

Complex cases

There are many complex referencing cases that this chapter does not cover. For example, you could be referencing two sources with the same author in the same year, which would create confusion in your in-text citations. Or you could be referencing two different sources with 4/5 of the same authors. This book is not designed to cover these complex cases so, if you are in doubt, please check with your faculty about a particular reference or citation. If you send your instructor a quick email with your question, not only will you receive an answer directly from the person who is marking your essay (meaning you have proof it is correct), but they may also be delighted to see your proactive approach towards academic honesty and referencing.

CHAPTER NINE: ESSAY FORMATTING

Introduction

Congratulations. You have planned, written, edited, and correctly referenced your essay. The final step is now formatting. It should always be done last, as it arranges your work into an organised, standard format.

Essay format refers to the following components: font size, font style, line spacing, headings, margins, page numbers, title, and alignment.

Depending on your university, course, professor, and assignment you may be required to use a particular style. All the referencing styles listed above have an overarching format that organises the whole essay, not just the reference list. It is very likely that your essay style will be the same as your referencing style. Therefore, if you are referencing in Harvard you can use our Harvard style guide to format your whole essay. This section will discuss the essay formats of Harvard, APA, and MLA.

- **Pro Tip**: Look out for those awkward professors out there who may ask you to use a different or bespoke formatting style than your referencing style suggests. In this case, we suggest you just listen to them.

Whilst we haven't included direct examples here, we have created templates that you can download at www.currikula.com/ultimate-essay-guide-resources

Harvard

Like the reference list, the Harvard essay format has very specific criteria. Below is a snapshot of criteria.

Font: Times New Roman size 12

Spacing: Double

Header: Shortened title followed by page number both justified right. Exactly five spaces between title and page number. Use 'View Master' header template in word to easily justify right.

Alignment: Align left only. No extra spaces between paragraphs. New paragraphs have an indentation. New heading when changing major topics.

Title page: FULL ESSAY TITLE IN ALL CAPS appears halfway down page. Three lines below is the name of the student (lower case letters). Four lines below the student is the course name. One line below course is the name of the professor. One line below is the name of the institution. One line below is the location of the institution. One line below is the date.

Margins: 1 inch margins on all sides

Title: Centred above first paragraph

APA

APA has some similarities to Harvard, such as a cover page. However, there are some subtle differences, such as the header and format of the title page. Please see below.

Font: Times New Roman size 12 recommended

Spacing: Double

Header: Page number justified right. Shortened title in ALL CAPS justified left.

Alignment: Align left only. No extra spaces between paragraphs. New paragraphs have an indentation. New heading when changing major topics.

Title page: Full Essay Title without full caps appears a third of the way down page, justified centre. One line below title is author. One line below author is university. The header on title page includes 'Running Head' before the shortened title. For example – Running head: THE SHORTENED ESSAY TITLE. After the title page 'Running head' is not included in the header. To accomplish this, click 'Options' when editing the header and select 'different first page'.

Margins: 1 inch margins on all sides

Title: Centred above first paragraph.

MLA

Unlike Harvard and APA, MLA does not require a cover or title page. The goal for the MLA style is standardisation, to focus attention on the actual writing of the essay rather than presentation. It is meant to be easier.

Font: Times New Roman size 12

Spacing: Double

Header: Author/student last name followed by page number. One space between author last name and page number. If required, replace author name with student number.

Title page: Not required

Heading info: Author full name or student number, instructor, course title, and date. Each piece of Information should be on a separate line double spaced and justified left.

Title: Centred above first paragraph.

ABOUT THE AUTHORS

Sam Loyd

Sam studied Philosophy at university and spent far more time trying to figure out how he could write good essays as fast as possible rather than blindly studying the old fashioned way. He perfected his system just in time for his thesis, which he got a high First Class in after writing it in just a week.

Justin Moryto

Justin studied Management with Marketing at the University of Exeter, where he wrote over 10,000 words per term of essays in multiple formatting and referencing styles. His distaste for unnecessary tasks led him to find the paths of least resistance when writing.

Together they both founded Currikula, an education based start-up aimed at helping students get better grades by improving the whole essay process. If you want to find out more, check out www.currikula.com.

Printed in Great Britain
by Amazon